The ESSENTIALS® of

Political Science

Anita C. Danker, M.A., M.Ed.
Social Studies Instructor
Hopkinton Jr/Sr High School, Hopkinton, MA

Research & Education Association
61 Ethel Road West
Piscataway, New Jersey 08854

THE ESSENTIALS®
OF POLITICAL SCIENCE

Printed in the United States of America

Library of Congress Control Number 2003103934

International Standard Book Number 0-87891-791-8

ESSENTIALS is a registered trademark of
Research & Education Association, Piscataway, New Jersey 08854

WHAT "THE ESSENTIALS" WILL DO FOR YOU

This book is a review and study guide. It is comprehensive and it is concise.

It helps in preparing for exams and in doing homework, and remains a handy reference source at all times.

It condenses the vast amount of detail characteristic of the subject matter and summarizes the **essentials** of the field.

It will thus save hours of study and preparation time.

The book provides quick access to the important facts, principles, statements, concepts, and theories in the field.

Materials needed for exams, can be reviewed in summary form—eliminating the need to read and re-read many pages of textbook and class notes. The summaries will even tend to bring detail to mind that had been previously read or noted.

This "ESSENTIALS" book has been prepared by an expert in the field and has been carefully reviewed to ensure its accuracy and maximum usefulness.

Dr. Max Fogiel
Program Director

CONTENTS

Chapter 3
UNITED STATES GOVERNMENT AND POLITICS

Chapter 4
COMPARATIVE GOVERNMENT AND POLITICS

Chapter 5
INTERNATIONAL RELATIONS

CHAPTER 1

Introduction to Political Science

1.1 Definitions

Political Science is the organized study of government and politics. It borrows from the related disciplines of history, philosophy, sociology, economics, and law. Political scientists explore such fundamental questions as: What are the philosophical foundations of modern political systems? What makes a government legitimate? What are the duties and responsibilities of those who govern? Who participates in the political process and why? What is the nature of relations among nations?

1.2 Principal Subfields of Political Science

At the present time, the study of political science in the United States is concerned with the following broad subtopics or subfields:

Political Theory – an historical exploration of the major contributions to political thought from the ancient Greeks to the contemporary theorists. These theorists raise fundamental questions about the individual's existence and his relationship to the political community. **Political theory** also involves the philosophical and speculative consideration of the political world.

American Government and Politics – a survey of the origins and development of the political system in the United States from the colonial days to modern times with an emphasis on the Constitution, various political structures such as the legislative, executive, and judicial branches, along with the federal system and political parties, voter behavior, and fundamental freedoms.

Comparative Government – a systematic study of the structures of two or more political systems (such as those of Britain and the People's Republic of China) to achieve an understanding of how different societies manage the realities of governing. Also considered are political processes and behavior and the ideological foundations of various systems.

International Relations – a consideration of how nations interact with each other within the frameworks of law, diplomacy, and international organizations such as the United Nations.

1.3 The Development of the Discipline of Political Science

Early History

Political science as a systematic study of government developed in the United States and in Western Europe during the Nineteenth Century as new political institutions evolved. Prior to 1850, during its classical phase, political science relied heavily on philosophy and utilized the deductive method of research.

Post–Civil War Period

The political science curriculum was formalized in the United States by faculty at Columbia and Johns Hopkins who were deeply influenced by German scholarship on the nation state and the formation of democratic institutions. Historical and comparative approaches to analysis of institutions were predominant. Emphasis was on constitutional and legal issues, and political institutions were widely regarded as factors in motivating the actions of individuals.

Twentieth Century Trends

Political scientists worked to strengthen their research base, to integrate quantitative data, and to incorporate into the discipline comparative studies of governmental structures in developing countries.

1.3.1 American Political Science Association (APSA)

The APSA was founded in 1903 to promote the organized study of politics and to distinguish it as a field separate from history.

1.3.2 The Behavioral Period

From the early 1920s to the present, political science has focused on psychological interpretations and the analysis of the behavior of individuals and groups in a political context. Research has been theory based, values neutral, and concerned with predicting and explaining political behavior.

1.3.3 Contemporary Developments

Since the 1960s, interest has focused on such subtopics as African American politics, public policy, urban and ethnic politics, and women in politics. Influenced by the leadership of Harold Lasswell, political scientists showed greater concern for using their discipline to solve social problems.

1.4 The Scientific Method of Research in Political Science

The modern method of scientific inquiry in the field aims to compile a body of data based on direct observation (**empirical knowledge**) that can be utilized both to explain what has been observed and to form valid generalizations. The scientific method in political science has resulted in three types of statements: **observational/evidential**, which describe the principal characteristics of what has been studied; **observational laws**, which are hypotheses based on what has been observed; and **theories**, which analyze the data that has been collected and offer plausible general principles that can be drawn from what has been observed.

1.4.1 Examples of Statements Based on the Scientific Method

- **Observational/evidential:** In 1992, 518 out of 535 members of the US Congress were males. In the British Parliament,

550 of the 635 members were males. Eighteen of France's 20 cabinet ministers were males.

- **Observational law (hypothesis):** Legislative and executive bodies in modern democracies tend to be dominated by males.

- **Theory:** Political power in modern democracies is in male hands.

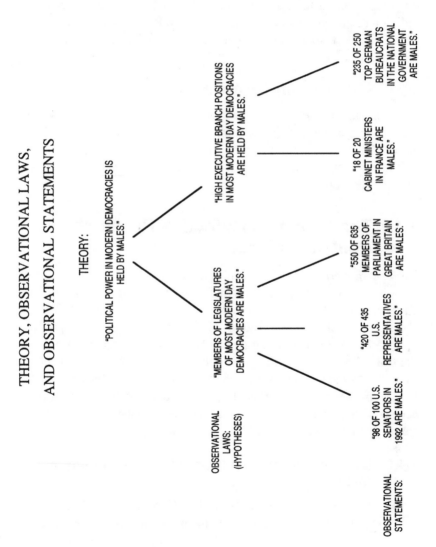

THEORY, OBSERVATIONAL LAWS, AND OBSERVATIONAL STATEMENTS

THEORY:

"POLITICAL POWER IN MODERN DEMOCRACIES IS HELD BY MALES."

OBSERVATIONAL LAWS: (HYPOTHESES)

"MEMBERS OF LEGISLATURES OF MOST MODERN DAY DEMOCRACIES ARE MALES."

"HIGH EXECUTIVE BRANCH POSITIONS IN MOST MODERN DAY DEMOCRACIES ARE HELD BY MALES."

OBSERVATIONAL STATEMENTS:

"98 OF 100 U.S. SENATORS IN 1992 ARE MALES."

"420 OF 435 U.S. REPRESENTATIVES ARE MALES."

"550 OF 635 MEMBERS OF PARLIAMENT IN GREAT BRITAIN ARE MALES."

"18 OF 20 CABINET MINISTERS IN FRANCE ARE MALES."

"235 OF 250 TOP GERMAN BUREAUCRATS IN THE NATIONAL GOVERNMENT ARE MALES."

4

CHAPTER 2

Political Theory

2.1   Ancient Greek Theorists (mid 400s – late 300s BC)

Plato's *Republic* may be considered the seminal essay on the nature of the state and the maintenance of political harmony. The Athenian philosopher describes an ideal society where justice prevails at the hands of wise rulers, philosopher kings. Order is secured by the guardians who are wholeheartedly devoted to the interests of their country. The workers - farmers, shepherds, and artisans - provide the material necessities. Friction is avoided by each class attending to its own business.

In *The Politics*, Plato's fellow Athenian and younger contemporary Aristotle describes man as a political animal and explores three principal forms of government: monarchy (rule by one), aristocracy (rule by the few), and polity (rule by the many). He deems the best political communities to be those comprised of members of a large middle class and warns against the tyrannies that can arise when a few possess great wealth (i.e. oligarchy) and the others little (i.e. democracy). Aristotle counsels that the key to maintaining the stability of the government is the education of the young in the habits and virtues of the society.

2.2　The Christian Scholars

After the fall of Rome and into the medieval period, Christian scholars sought to reconcile the classical philosophical writings of the ancient Greeks with the theological doctrines of the Christian church. Two figures were of paramount importance in this mission: **St. Augustine** (354–430 AD) and **St. Thomas Aquinas** (circa 1226–1274).

In his multivolume *City of God*, Augustine envisions two cities - one of this world and the other, God's city, in heaven. To Augustine, the symbol of the heavenly city is the church, and the earthly city is embodied in the state. The state must maintain peace and order so that human beings can lead lives that will obtain them access to the heavenly city. Justice is a key concept in Augustine's writings. It can only be attained after mortals enter into a proper relationship with God. Augustine is credited with taking Plato's concept of justice and imbuing it with a religious cast.

Where Augustine is associated with adapting Plato's thought to Christian teachings, Aquinas is credited with highlighting and transforming the philosophical tenets of Aristotle. Aquinas' work belongs to a body of scholarship called **scholasticism**, an attempt to align the teachings of the church with the realms of science and reason. His principal contribution, *Summa Theologica*, explores such basic political questions as:

- How is law related to reason?
- Is law created for the good of all?
- What is the relationship between human and natural law?
- Is a state better off governed by one or by many rulers?

Aquinas maintains that rulers are charged with three primary responsibilities: to show concern for the good of the masses so that the state may continue its existence, to lead the people in the ways of virtue, and to protect their subjects from enemy attacks.

2.3 Secularism

The theological framework from which the medieval scholars operated was challenged by the re-awakened interest in the classical world and cultural rebirth that characterized the period in Western civilization known as the **Renaissance**. Spanning the Fourteenth and Sixteenth Centuries, this era was marked by a rejection of the religious preoccupation of the medieval theorists and an increased emphasis on man and the business of this world, not the hereafter (**secularism**).

A key figure in the realm of the realistic political theory of the Renaissance was **Niccolo Machiavelli** (1469–1527) of Florence. A public servant and diplomat, Machiavelli was exiled for several years when the Medici family assumed power in 1512; Machiavelli was later restored to favor. His major contribution, *The Prince* (1513), which is dedicated to Lorenzo de Medici, is considered the first modern work of political philosophy. Unlike medieval tracts, with their reliance on religious authority, *The Prince* eschews moral and ethical considerations and examines the political realities of the times at hand. Machiavelli is primarily concerned with power and how rulers gain and maintain it. Among Machiavelli's fundamental components of effective leadership are: 1) a willingness to imitate the behavior of great men; 2) the ability to illustrate how government is necessary to the well-being of the populace; 3) a dedication to the art of war; 4) an understanding that apparent cruelties and vices may be essential to maintaining stability and power; 5) prudence with respect to disbursement of one's own wealth; and 6) the wisdom to seek advice and counsel only when it is needed. Though closely associated with the maxims that for a ruler "it is better to be feared than loved" and that in governance the "end justifies the means," Machiavelli does caution that wise rulers must avoid being hated and must strive to appear to be and indeed *be* virtuous and just whenever possible.

2.4 Theorists of the Enlightenment

The Eighteenth Century is referred to as the "age of reason" or the **Enlightenment**. It was an era of progress and optimism during

7

which advances were made in economics, education, government, philosophy, religion, and science that were characteristically modern in flavor. In general there was a belief in reason as the key to perfection and as the basis for unraveling the complexities of natural law. In the realm of political theory, the **Baron de Montesquieu** (1689–1755) and **Jean-Jacques Rousseau** (1712–1778) were among the most distinguished. An earlier theorist, **Thomas Hobbes** (1588–1679), provided seminal ideas with respect to the darker side of human nature upon which the concept of the **social contract** was built. **John Locke** (1632–1704), a supporter of Britain's Glorious Revolution of 1688, expanded on the social contract and helped to lay the intellectual foundations of the Enlightenment. These philosophers provided a theoretical framework for the American Revolution, although the pessimism of Hobbes was largely rejected by the Founding Fathers.

British royalist Hobbes, a mathematician, tutor, and philosopher, authored *Leviathan* (1651), an analysis of human nature, the character of the state, and the concept of sovereignty. Negative in tone, *Leviathan* asserts that human beings are competitive, acquisitive, and quarrelsome. They desire peace only because they fear death and enter into covenants (**social contracts**) with other individuals for purposes of mutual security. The most efficient form of government in the Hobbes schema is an absolute monarchy because it unites private with public interest and bypasses the inconveniences of divided opinion, envy, and faction that punctuate assemblies. Whatever the style of government under consideration, Hobbes stresses the absolute nature and power of the sovereign, be it an individual or a collective body.

John Locke, author of the influential works *Two Treatises of Government* (1689) and *Essay Concerning Human Understanding* (1690), originated the concept of the **tabula rasa** (the mind at birth is a blank slate, and all knowledge is the result of experience) and is regarded as the founder of the liberal school of philosophical thought. Building on Hobbes' framework of the social contract, Locke denied the legitimacy of **divine right** (the belief that the right of sovereigns to govern emanates from God) and promulgated the concepts of individual freedom and rule by the consent of the governed that permeate the founding documents of the United States. John Locke's greatest claim to fame regarding the natural rights doctrine was his recognition that when people's natural rights to life, liberty, and estate (property) were violated or endangered, the oppressed had the ultimate right to "appeal to Heaven"—i.e., the right to revolution to redress their grievances. This was to become the ideological cornerstone of the Declaration of Independence.

French Enlightenment theorist, the Baron de Montesquieu, was influenced by the British parliamentary system and Locke's defense of it. His *Spirit of the Laws* (1748) argues for **separation of powers** (the division of government into legislative, executive, and judicial branches) and **checks and balances** (a system whereby one branch can limit the power of the others). Regarded as middle-of-the-road in thought, Montesquieu condemned tyranny and despotism while accepting monarchy as a legitimate system of government for some states. He saw such factors as culture, economics, and geography as determinants of which type of government might best suit a particular society. Montesquieu's moderate doctrines are clearly evident in the United States Constitution.

While Montesquieu was flexible in his approach to reform, fellow French philosopher Jean-Jacques Rousseau was adamant in his support of a radical program for political change. His emphasis on the well-being of society over the rights of the individual is apparent in the *Social Contract* (1762) in which he argues for the sovereignty of the general will and majority rule. Rousseau's call for direct democracy and freedom marked him as one of the Enlightenment's most radical reformers.

2.5 Early Modern Political Thinkers

In the late stages of the Eighteenth Century, the first distinctly modern political thinkers emerged. Their writings paralleled the evolution of the nation-state and were concerned with creating a blueprint for the most humane and desirable political system. Among the most influential of the early moderns were the **Marquis de Condorcet** (1743–1794), a French reformer, and the German philosopher, **Immanuel Kant** (1724–1804).

A mathematician and humanitarian who advocated an end to

both slavery and the death penalty, Condorcet went into hiding during the excesses of the French Revolution and wrote his *Sketch for a Historical Picture of the Progress of the Human Mind* (1793–1794) as he sought to escape the guillotine. In this optimistic work, Condorcet traces history as a progressive voyage culminating in a future where the concepts of reason, equality, and individual rights prevail. He predicts unbounded progress in the scientific as well as in the moral and political spheres, hence he is regarded as a quintessential Western theorist.

Kant's writings explore the concepts of moral law and **autonomy of will**. He is recognized for originating the idea of the **categorical imperative**—that is, moral law that instructs individuals to act out of a sense of duty on the basis of what is right. The idea of law is central to Kant's vision, for only under conditions of regulation can the wills of all individuals be joined harmoniously. He equates autonomy with freedom, but in order for the general populace to experience freedom, each individual in society must surrender a measure of personal liberty for the benefit of all. Kant's modernism is manifest in his emphasis on the dignity of humankind, equality before the law, due process, universal education, and world peace.

2.6 Products of the Eighteenth Century Revolutions

The American and French revolutions of the Eighteenth Century sparked a body of political philosophy that both supported and rejected their principles and results. **Edmund Burke** (1729–1797), a conservative, **Thomas Paine** (1737–1809), a republican, and **Joseph De Maistre** (1753–1821), a reactionary, were representative political theorists of the period.

Burke, the defender of Britain's parliamentary government, supported the political party as a means of promoting the interests of the state and at the same time accepted the aristocracy as the critical component in maintaining the social order. In 1790, he published his major work, *Reflections on the Revolution in France*. Here he attacks most of the fundamental principles that motivated the overthrow of the *ancien regime* including the concepts of individual rights, equality, and revolution as a vehicle for change. Burke argues for a preservation of the existing order and of the political institutions that perpetuate the stability of that order.

Paine, on the other hand, called for bold action to redress grievances against governments and was instrumental in precipitating the American call for independence and subsequent military action against the British. Paine wrote *Common Sense* (1776), a pamphlet that encouraged the break with England on practical as well as ideological grounds. His *The Rights of Man* (1791) is a counterpoint to Burke's *Reflections* and a spirited defense of the French Revolution. Paine argues for the right of nations to discard outmoded institutions and to undertake the creation of more effective ones. His favored mode of government is the republic for its protection of both the public interest and individual rights.

Where Paine espoused revolutions and republics, De Maistre darkly focused on the violent nature of the human race and the need for terror as an instrument of control. Despotism and absolutism are inevitable in De Maistre's vision, which sees reason, progress, and perfectibility, the goals of the Enlightenment, as spurious and unattainable. De Maistre contributed to the development of political science as a discipline with his emphasis on accumulating data and applying the scientific method social phenomena.

2.7   Romantics and Idealists

In the Nineteenth Century, a reaction developed in response to the rational-intellectual, scientific, and industrial currents that seemed to prevail. One manifestation of this reaction was seen in the code of the **romantics**, who stressed the importance of passion, spiritualism, and impulse in the arts and in all forms of self-expression. Closely related to romanticism is **idealism**, a German school of philosophy that emphasizes the mind and the spirit as paramount. Key figures in these movements were **Thomas Carlyle** (1795–1881), an historian of the romantic school, and **Friedrich Hegel** (1797–1831), who developed a strand of history based on idealism.

Carlyle, who is best known for popularizing the "great man" approach to history, mistrusted democracy and deemed the aristocracy to be most able to lead politically. Wary of both the plutocrats who revered money and the masses who worshipped liberty, Carlyle was troubled by both the industrial and political revolutions of his age. Deeply impacted by the German idealists, he spread their ideas to his English audiences.

The most influential of the German idealists was Friedrich Hegel, who generated the proposition that history is an idea that develops through a **dialectical** process (thesis/idea > antithesis > synthesis). Each stage of history is flawed as cultures engage in conflict and war in their efforts to dominate. Hegel glorified Prussia as one of the nations responsible for energizing the progressive movement of history.

2.8   The Utilitarians

This group of largely British theorists believed in the practical dictum that choices that produce positive results are best. Translated into policy, utilitarianism generated a number of Nineteenth Century reforms in the fields of economics, education, law, and politics that were both liberal and humane. Leading utilitarian thinkers included **Jeremy Bentham** (1748–1832), and **Adam Smith** (1723–1790).

Bentham is generally recognized as the founder of the utilitarian school of philosophy with his **"greatest happiness principle."** By this Bentham meant that the best policy is one that avoids the most pain and brings the most pleasure to the greatest number. He based his conclusions on systematic inquiry into the nature of humankind which he saw as basically a pleasure-seeking race. The principal task of government, according to Bentham, is to promote the well-being of its citizenry through a system of rewards and consequences. Lawmakers must set about leading others to act on behalf of others as well as for themselves.

Economist Adam Smith published his classic *Wealth of Nations* in 1776 in which he argued for a laissez-faire approach with respect to governments and matters of business and commerce. As a utilitarian, Smith believed that each individual would act in his/her own self-interest, and, in so doing, would benefit the society as a whole. The self-interest of individuals would act as an **invisible hand** to guide the economy, which should operate under conditions of market competition and free trade.

The pragmatic utilitarians with their pursuit-of-pleasure emphasis engendered a reaction that resulted in systematic critical analysis expressed by **John Stuart Mill** (1806–1873). To Mill, life was more than a mindless quest for pleasure. A champion of liberty and free speech, Mill underscored the importance of good character, artistic expression, interpersonal relations, and social conscience. Mill's ideal government would be an instrument of education and elevation through which citizens raise standards and display their public spirit.

2.9   The Aristocratic Conservatives

As the Nineteenth Century reforms proliferated, critics expressed the fear that sovereignty was shifting to those least able to ensure the stability of the state, the masses. Conservatives in both Europe and the United States called for a curb on these tendencies and presented a somewhat dark view of the future. Leading spokespersons in this camp were French aristocrat **Alexis de Tocqueville** (1805–1859) and American historian **Henry Adams** (1839–1918).

The result of a voyage to the United States in 1832, ostensibly to study the American penal system, *Democracy in America* (1835) was published by Tocqueville and has since been regarded as a classic study of government based on the will of the people. Tocqueville expressed an uneasiness about democratic institutions with their insistence on equality, for he feared this emphasis could ultimately lead to a destruction of freedom and a climate of mediocrity. His warnings as to the consequences of a preoccupation with material gain and the dangers of a "tyranny of the majority" were well taken. Tocqueville's preferred plan of government would avoid centralization and would recognize the value of local institutions.

Henry Adams, the son of a family of statesmen and presidents, saw his own life as an unfulfilled quest for knowledge and wisdom.

In his widely-read *The Education of Henry Adams* (1907), he underscores a social and political system in the United States that stifles creativity and rewards incompetence. Adams pessimistically described history as in a continuous process of decline and predicted the ultimate disintegration of democracy.

2.10 The Nationalists

This group of theorists explained and defended the Nineteenth Century drive to unite ethnic populations (i.e. Germany and Italy) and to achieve both liberation and independence. A leading spokesperson for this point of view was the Italian patriot, **Giuseppe Mazzini** (1805–1872). He was deeply involved in the movement for Italian unification and related this process to other nations as well. He taught that national groups were responsible for effecting their own independence. Anti-monarchist in sentiment, Mazzini believed in popular sovereignty and democracy as the currents of the future.

2.10.1 Ethnic Nationalism

In the late stages of the Nineteenth Century and throughout the twentieth century, nationalism has focused less on geographic unity and more on race as the defining characteristic of nation states. Three examples of this trend include:

> **Zionism** – a drive to unite the Jews scattered throughout the world in an independent Palestine, the historical homeland of the people of Israel.

> **Nazism** – associated with Twentieth Century dictator **Adolf Hitler** (1889–1945) and developed in his *Mein Kampf* (1924), this doctrine asserted the racial superiority of pure Germans (Aryans) and called for a national policy that was anti-Semitic, militaristic, and imperialistic. Nazism mandated a rigid system of control over the lives of individual citizens (totalitarianism).

> **Ethnic Cleansing** – displacement and mass murder taking place in the former Yugoslavia in the 1990s following the collapse of Soviet hegemony.

2.11 Social Darwinists

These philosophers applied Darwin's theory of evolution to society and claimed that such concepts as natural selection and survival of the fittest could explain human behavior and social stratification. In general they advocated control as a mechanism to keep "inferior" peoples from proliferating. In the economic sphere, the Social Darwinists championed competition and capitalism. Society overall would benefit from competitive struggles because in the end the most fit would prevail. The most influential representative of the Social Darwinists was **Herbert Spencer** (1820–1903), a British social philosopher.

Spencer's *Social Statics* (1850) sets forth the principles that eventually formed the basis of Social Darwinism. Here Spencer describes the march of civilization as an evolutionary process from a simple to an ever more complex world. Humans must adjust to a constantly changing society, and government's role is to remain on the sidelines. Efforts to legislate social welfare policies are unwise because they interfere with the natural process of the survival of the fittest.

2.11.1 Nietzsche's Irrationalism

Not classified as a Social Darwinist, yet sympathetic to their glorification of strength, was **Friedrich Nietzsche** (1844–1900). As an **irrationalist,** Nietzsche rejected the artificiality of empirical approaches and stressed the role of myth and conflict in developing civilizations. His *Thus Spake Zarathustra* (1892) sets forth a world view that rejects weakness, emphasizes the concept of the will to power, and embraces the dictum that strong leadership is a necessity. Nietzsche's philosophy has been linked to the nationalistic music of Richard Wagner and the racist doctrines of Adolf Hitler.

2.12 Marxists, Socialists, and Anarchists

While liberals and conservatives concerned themselves with questions of freedom and individual liberty, a major philosophical school born in the industrial displacement of the Nineteenth Century analyzed questions of history and public policy from the perspective of the good of society. The most influential of the socialist theorists was

Karl Marx (1818–1883), the father of modern communism. In reaction to the revolutionary principles of Marxism and the statism of planned economic and political systems, two counterstrands developed, **democratic socialism** and **anarchism**.

In his revolutionary treatise, *The Communist Manifesto* (1848), written in conjunction with **Friedrich Engels**, as well as in the voluminous *Das Kapital* (1867, 1885, and 1894), Marx originates a series of doctrines that underscore economics as the critical factor in shaping history. Like Hegel, Marx stresses the dialectical procession of historical development. Grounded in his observation of the excesses of the industrial revolution in Great Britain, Marx's theories identify unbridled capitalism as an evil that concentrates wealth in the hands of the few and deprives the masses of a decent life. He predicts the revolution of the working class (**proletariat**) and the eventual transfer of political power into their grasp.

Twentieth-century Marxists included partners in the Bolshevik revolution in Russia, **V. I. Lenin** (1870–1924) and **Leon Trotsky** (1879–1940). Lenin adapted Marxist doctrines to the realities of revolutionary Russia in 1917. He headed the successful Bolshevik uprising in an underdeveloped, largely peasant society unlike the industrial state Marx targeted as the logical starting point for socialist upheaval. In *What Is to Be Done?* (1902), Lenin presents his argument that a small, highly disciplined party elite is capable of leading a successful rebellion. Trotsky, though Lenin's ally in the revolution, disagreed with the latter in his concept of party. His contribution to Marxist doctrine lies in his advocacy of a permanent state of revolution on an international scale. Exiled under **Stalin**, Trotsky wrote *The Revolution Betrayed* (1936) which was highly critical of Stalinism. He was murdered in 1940, most probably under orders from Stalin.

In contrast to the totalitarianism that accompanied the institutionalization of socialism in Russia is the strand practiced in Scandinavia and Great Britain. Labeled **democratic socialism**, this system provides for the welfare of its workers through government-operated health, housing, educational, and transportation arrangements.

Both Marxism and democratic socialism require strong central authorities to plan and effect welfare policies. A political philosophy diametrically opposed to state control is **anarchism**. Adherents of this doctrine seek to eliminate the state in order to allow individuals to pursue their economic and personal lives free from the restraints of government-imposed regulations and bureaucratic coercion.

2.13 Twentieth Century Economic and Social Theorists

Political theory in the twentieth century has been more closely linked with economics and sociology than with history, as was the case in the past. Two modern political theorists who are representative of this trend are **Max Weber** (1864–1920), a German social scientist, and British political science professor, **Harold Laski** (1893–1950).

Weber's classic, *The Protestant Ethic and the Spirit of Capitalism* (1904), links religious and economic themes in its argument that Calvinism, with its insistence on hard-work and frugality, was the principal force responsible for the development of capitalism. An analyst of bureaucratic institutions, Weber denounced their proliferation in his beloved Germany. He admired the United States and praised its democratic tendencies. Weber argued that governments should develop programs friendly to the working class and at the same time maintain strong foreign policies.

Somewhat inconsistent in his views, Laski espoused the doctrine of **political pluralism**, a system that defended the rights of groups such as labor unions to be served, not dominated, by the state. Later he shifted his emphasis to individual liberty which is identified with classical liberalism. Finally, with the rise of Fascism in Europe, Laski developed a sympathy for the doctrines of Marxian socialism.

CHAPTER 3

United States Government and Politics

3.1 Constitutional Foundations

The government of the United States rests on a written framework created in an attempt to strengthen a loose confederation that was in crisis in the 1780s. The **Constitution** is a basic plan that outlines the structure and functions of the national government. Clearly rooted in Western political thought, it sets limits and protects both property and individual rights.

3.1.1 Historical Background

Following the successful revolt of the British colonies in North America against imperial rule, a plan of government was implemented that was consciously weak and ultimately ineffective, the **Articles of Confederation**. The Articles served as the national government from 1781–1787. The government under the Articles consisted of a **unicameral** (one house) legislature which was clearly subordinate to the states. Representatives to the Congress were appointed and paid by their respective state legislatures, and their mission was to protect the interests of their home states. Each state, regardless of size, had one vote in Congress, which could request but not require states to provide financial and military support. **Key weak-**

nesses of the Articles included: its inability to regulate interstate and foreign trade, its lack of a chief executive and a national court system, and its rule that amendments must be approved by unanimous consent.

Dubbed the "**critical period**," the 1780s was a decade in the United States marked by internal conflict. The economy deteriorated as individual states printed their own currencies, taxed the products of their neighbors, and ignored foreign trade agreements. Inflation soared, small farmers lost their property, and states engaged in petty squabbles with one another. The discontent of the agrarian population reached crisis proportions in 1786 in rural Massachusetts when Revolutionary War veteran **Daniel Shays** led a rebellion of farmers against the tax collectors and the banks that were seizing their property. **Shays' Rebellion** symbolized the inability of the government under the Articles to maintain order. If anything, Shays' Rebellion (1786–1787) reflected the confederation of states' inability to raise and support an army (another key weakness).

In response to the economic and social disorder and the dangers of foreign intervention, a series of meetings to consider reform of the Articles was held. In 1787, the **Constitutional Convention** was convened in **Philadelphia** ostensibly to revise the ineffective Articles. The result was an entirely new plan of government, the Constitution.

3.1.2   Philosophy and Ideology of the Founding Fathers

Among the distinguished men assembled at the Constitutional Convention in 1787 were **James Madison**, who recorded the debate proceedings; **George Washington**, president of the body; **Gouverneur Morris**, who wrote the final version of the document, and **Alexander Hamilton**, one of the authors of the *Federalist Papers* (1787–1788). This collection of essays, to which **Madison** and **John Jay** also contributed, expresses the political philosophy of the Founders and was instrumental in bringing about the ratification of the Constitution.

Clearly the framers of the Constitution were influenced by the ideological heritage of the Seventeenth and Eighteenth Century Enlightenment in Western Europe. From Hobbes and Locke came the concept of the social contract. The latter had a marked influence

19

upon **Thomas Jefferson**, who incorporated Locke's doctrines with respect to equality; government's responsibility to protect the life, liberty, and property of its constituency; and the right of revolution in his **Declaration of Independence** (1776). The Constitution itself includes Montesquieu's separation of powers and checks and balances. British documents such as the **Magna Carta** (1215), the **Petition of Right** (1628), and the **Bill of Rights** (1689), all promoting the principle of limited government, were influential in shaping the final form of the Constitution.

3.1.3 Basic Principles of the Constitution

The authors of the Constitution sought to establish a government free from the tyrannies of both monarchs and mobs. Two of the critical principles embedded in the final document, **federalism** and **separation of powers**, address this concern.

The federal system established by the Founders divides the powers of government between the states and the national government. Local matters are handled on a local level, and those issues that affect the general populace are the responsibility of the federal government. Such a system is a natural outgrowth of the colonial relationship between the Americans and the mother country of England. American federalism is defined in the **Tenth Amendment** which declares: "those powers not delegated to the United States by the Constitution, nor prohibited by it to the States, are reserved to the States respectively, or to the people." In practice, the system may be confusing in that powers overlap (i.e. welfare). In cases where they conflict, the federal government is supreme.

The principle of separation of powers is codified in **Articles I, II**, and **III** of the main body of the Constitution. The national government is divided into three branches which have separate functions (**legislative**, **executive**, and **judicial**). Not entirely independent, each of these branches can check or limit in some way the power of one or both of the others (**checks and balances**). This system of dividing and checking powers is a vehicle for guarding against the extremes the Founders feared. Following are some examples of checks and balances:

- The legislative branch can check the executive by refusing to confirm appointments.

- The executive can check the legislative by vetoing its bills.

- The judicial can check both the legislative and the executive by declaring laws unconstitutional.

Additional basic principles embodied in the Constitution include:

- The establishment of a representative government (**republic**).

- **Popular sovereignty** or the idea that government derives its power from the people. This concept is expressed in the **Preamble** which opens with the words, "**We the People**."

- The enforcement of government with limits ("**rule of law**").

3.2 Structure and Functions of the National Government

The national government consists of the three branches outlined in the Constitution as well as a huge bureaucracy comprised of departments, agencies, and commissions.

3.2.1 The Legislative Branch

Legislative power is vested in a **bicameral** (two-house) Congress which is the subject of Article I of the Constitution. The bicameral structure was the result of a compromise at the Constitutional Convention between the large states, led by Virginia, which presented a plan calling for a strong national government with representation favoring the larger states (**Virginia Plan**) and the smaller states, which countered with the **New Jersey Plan**. The latter would have retained much of the structure of the Articles of Confederation including equal representation of the states in Congress. Connecticut offered a solution in the form of the **Great Compromise**. It called for a two-house legislature with equal representation in the **Senate** and representation in the **House of Representatives** based on population.

The **expressed** or **delegated powers** of Congress are set forth in **Section 8** of Article I. They can be divided into several broad categories including economic, judicial, war, and general peace powers. **Economic powers** include:

- to lay and collect taxes
- to borrow money
- to regulate foreign and interstate commerce
- to coin money and regulate its value
- to establish rules concerning bankruptcy

Judicial powers include:

- to establish courts inferior to the Supreme Court
- to provide punishment for counterfeiting
- to define and punish piracies and felonies committed on the high seas

War powers include:

- to declare war
- to raise and support armies
- to provide and maintain a navy
- to provide for organizing, arming, and calling forth the militia

Peace powers include:

- to establish rules on naturalization
- to establish post offices and post roads
- to promote science and the arts by granting patents and copyrights
- to exercise jurisdiction over the seat of the federal government (**District of Columbia**)

The Constitution includes the so-called **"elastic clause"** which grants Congress **implied powers** to implement the delegated powers.

In addition, Congress maintains the power to discipline federal officials through **impeachment** (formal accusation of wrongdoing) and removal from office.

Article V empowers Congress to propose **amendments** (changes or additions) to the Constitution. A two-thirds majority in both houses is necessary for passage. An alternate method is to have amendments proposed by the legislatures of two-thirds of the states. In order for an amendment to become part of the Constitution it must be **ratified** (formally approved) by three-fourths of the states (through their legislatures or by way of special conventions as in the case of the repeal of Prohibition).

Article I, Section 9 specifically denies certain powers to the national legislature. Congress is prohibited from suspending the right of **habeas corpus** (writ calling for a party under arrest to be brought before the court where authorities must show cause for detainment) except during war or rebellion. Other prohibitions include: the passage of export taxes, the withdrawal of funds from the treasury without an appropriations law, the passage of **ex post facto** laws (make past actions punishable that were legal when they occurred), and favored treatment of one state over another with respect to commerce.

The work of the Congress is organized around a committee system. The **standing committees** are permanent and deal with such matters as agriculture, the armed services, the budget, energy, finance, and foreign policy. Special or **select committees** are established to deal with specific issues and usually have a limited duration. **Conference committees** iron out differences between House and Senate versions of a bill before it is sent on to the President.

One committee unique to the House of Representatives is the powerful **Rules Committee**. Thousands of bills are introduced each term, and the Rules Committee acts as a clearing house to weed out those that are unworthy of consideration before the full House. Constitutionally, all revenue-raising bills must originate in the House of Representatives. They are scrutinized by the powerful House **Ways and Means Committee**.

Committee membership is organized on party lines with **seniority** being a key factor, although in recent years, length of service has diminished in importance in the determination of chairmanships. The composition of each committee is largely based on the ratio of each party in the Congress as a whole. The party that has a **majority** is allotted a greater number of members on each committee. The chairman of the standing committees are selected by the leaders of the majority party.

The legislative process is at once cumbersome and time-consuming (see chart **How A Bill Becomes A Law**). A **bill** (proposed law) can be introduced in either house (with the exception of **revenue bills**, which must originate in the House of Representatives). It is referred to the appropriate **committee** and then to a **subcommittee**, which will hold **hearings** if the members agree that it has merit. The bill is reported back to the **full committee**, which must decide whether or not to send it to the **full chamber** to be debated. If the bill passes in the full chamber, it is then sent to the **other chamber** to begin the process all over again. Any differences between the House and Senate versions of the bill must resolved in a **conference committee** before it is sent to the **President** for consideration. Most of the thousands of bills introduced in Congress die in committee with only a small percentage becoming law.

Debate on major bills is a key step in the legislative process because of the tradition of attaching **amendments** at this stage. In the House, the rules of debate are designed to enforce limits necessitated by the size of the body (435 members). In the smaller Senate (100 members), unlimited debate (**filibuster**) is allowed. Filibustering is a delaying tactic that can postpone action indefinitely. **Cloture** is a parliamentary procedure that can limit debate and bring a filibuster to an end.

Constitutional qualifications for the House of Representatives state that members must be at least **twenty-five** years of age, must have been **U.S. citizens for at least seven years**, and must be **residents of the state** that sends them to Congress. According to the **Reapportionment Act of 1929**, the size of the House is fixed at **435** members. They serve terms of **two years** in length. The presiding officer and generally the most powerful member is the **Speaker of the House**, who is the leader of the political party that has a majority in a given term.

Constitutional qualifications for the Senate state that a member must be at least **thirty** years of age, must have been a **U.S.**

HOW A BILL BECOMES A LAW

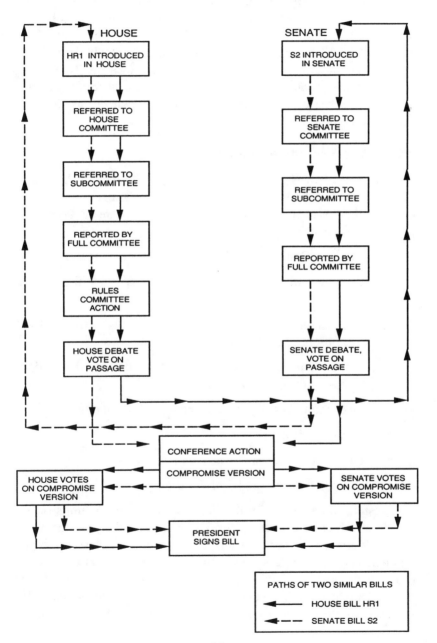

HOUSE

HR1 INTRODUCED IN HOUSE

REFERRED TO HOUSE COMMITTEE

REFERRED TO SUBCOMMITTEE

REPORTED BY FULL COMMITTEE

RULES COMMITTEE ACTION

HOUSE DEBATE VOTE ON PASSAGE

SENATE

S2 INTRODUCED IN SENATE

REFERRED TO SENATE COMMITTEE

REFERRED TO SUBCOMMITTEE

REPORTED BY FULL COMMITTEE

SENATE DEBATE, VOTE ON PASSAGE

CONFERENCE ACTION

COMPROMISE VERSION

HOUSE VOTES ON COMPROMISE VERSION

SENATE VOTES ON COMPROMISE VERSION

PRESIDENT SIGNS BILL

PATHS OF TWO SIMILAR BILLS

HOUSE BILL HR1

SENATE BILL S2

25

citizen for at least nine years, and must be an inhabitant of the state that he/she represents. Senators are elected for terms of six years in length on a staggered basis so that one-third of the body is up for re-election in each national election. The president of the Senate is the Vice-President. This role is largely symbolic, with the Vice-President casting a vote only in the case of a tie. There is no position in the Senate comparable to that of the Speaker of the House, although the majority leader is generally recognized as the most powerful member.

3.2.2 The Executive Branch

The President is the head of the executive branch of the federal government. Article II of the Constitution deals with the powers and duties of the President or chief executive. Following are the President's principal constitutional responsibilities:

- serves as Commander-in-Chief of the armed forces
- negotiates treaties (with the approval of two-thirds of the Senate)
- appoints ambassadors, judges, and other high officials (with the consent of the Senate)
- grants pardons and reprieves for those convicted of federal crimes (except in impeachment cases)
- seeks counsel of department heads (Cabinet members)
- recommends legislation
- meets with representatives of foreign states
- sees that the laws are faithfully executed

Despite the attempts by the Founders to set clear limits on the power of the chief executive, the importance of the presidency has grown dramatically over the years. Recent trends to reassert the pre-eminence of the Congress notwithstanding, the President remains the most visible and powerful single member of the federal government and the only one (with the exception of the Vice-President) elected to represent all the people. He shapes foreign policy with his diplomatic

26

and treaty-making powers and largely determines domestic policy. Presidents also possess the power to **veto** legislation. A presidential veto may be overridden by a two-thirds vote in both houses, but such a majority is not easy to build, particularly in the face of the chief executive's opposition. A **pocket veto** occurs when the President neither signs nor rejects a bill, and the Congress adjourns within ten days of his receipt of the legislation. The fact that the President is the head of a vast federal bureaucracy is another indication of the power of the office.

Although the Constitution makes no mention of a formal **Cabinet** as such, since the days of George Washington, chief executives have relied on department heads to aid in the decision-making process. Washington's Cabinet was comprised of the secretaries of **State**, **War**, **Treasury**, and an **Attorney-General**. Today there are fourteen Cabinet departments, with **Veterans' Affairs** the most recently created post. Efforts to trim the federal government in the 1990s have resulted in suggestions to streamline and eliminate some Cabinet posts.

The **Executive Office of the President** is made up of agencies that supervise the daily work of the government. The **White House Staff** manages the President's schedule and is usually headed by a powerful **chief of staff**. Arguably the most critical agency of the Executive Office is the **Office of Management and Budget**, which controls the budget process for the national government. Other key executive agencies include the **Council of Economic Advisors** and the **National Security Council**, which advises the President on matters that threaten the safety of the nation and directs the **Central Intelligence Agency**.

The **Constitutional Requirements** for the office of President and Vice-President are as follows: a candidate must be at least **thirty-five** years of age, must be a **natural-born** citizen, and must have **resided in the United States for a minimum of fourteen years**. Article II provides for an **Electoral College** to elect the President and Vice-President. Each state has as many votes in the Electoral College as it has members of Congress plus three additional electors from the District of Columbia—making a grand total of 538 electors. The Founding Fathers established the Electoral College to provide an

indirect method of choosing the chief executive, but over time the body has become ceremonial due to the control the major political parties have over the election process.

The question of **presidential succession** has been addressed by both legislation and amendment. The Constitution states that if the President dies or cannot perform his duties, the "powers and duties" of the office shall "devolve" on the Vice-President. The **Presidential Succession Act** (1947) placed the **Speaker of the House** next in line if both the President and the Vice-President were unable to serve. Until recently, when the Vice-President assumed the office of President, his former position was left vacant. The **Twenty-Fifth Amendment** (1967) gives the President the power to appoint a new Vice-President (with the approval of a majority of both houses of Congress). It also provides for the Vice-President to serve as **Acting President** if the chief executive is disabled or otherwise unable to carry out the duties of the office. The **Twenty-Second Amendment** (1951) limits the President's tenure to **two terms**.

3.2.3 The Judicial Branch

Article III of the Constitution establishes the **Supreme Court** but does not define the role of this branch as clearly as it does the legislative and executive branches. Yet our contemporary judicial branch consists of thousands of courts and is in essence a dual system with each state having its own judiciary functioning simultaneously with a complete set of federal courts. The most significant piece of legislation with respect to establishing a network of federal courts was the **Judiciary Act of 1789**. This law organized the Supreme Court and set up the thirteen **federal district courts**. The district courts have **original jurisdiction** (to hear cases in the first instance) for federal cases involving both civil and criminal law. Federal cases on appeal are heard in the **Courts of Appeal**. The decisions of these courts are final, except for those cases that are accepted for review by the Supreme Court.

The **Supreme Court** today is made of a **Chief Justice** and eight **Associate Justices**. They are appointed for life by the President with the approval of the Senate.

In the early history of the United States, the Supreme Court was largely preoccupied with the relationship between the federal government and those of the states. In 1803, the process of **judicial review** (power to determine the constitutionality of laws and actions of the legislative and executive branches) was established under **Chief Justice John Marshall** in the case of **Marbury v. Madison.** This power has become the foundation of the American judicial system and underscores the deep significance of the courts in determining the course of United States history.

The Supreme Court chooses cases for review based on whether or not they address substantial federal issues. If four of the nine justices vote to consider a case, then it will be added to the agenda. In such cases, **writs of certiorari** (orders calling up the records from a lower court) are issued. The justices are given detailed briefs and hear oral arguments. Reaching a decision is a complicated process. The justices scrutinize the case with reference to the Constitution and also consider previous decisions in similar cases (**precedent**). When all of the justices agree, the opinion issued is **unanimous.** In the case of a split decision, a **majority opinion** is written by one of the justices in agreement. Sometimes a justice will agree with the majority but for a different principle, in which case he/she can write a **concurring opinion** explaining the different point of view. Justices who do not vote with the majority may choose to write **dissenting opinions** to air their conflicting arguments.

In addition to the Supreme Court, the federal District Courts, and the Courts of Appeal, several special courts at the federal level have been created by Congress. The **U.S. Tax Court** handles conflicts between citizens and the Internal Revenue Service. The **Court of Claims** was designed to hear cases in which citizens bring suit against the U.S. government. Other special courts include the **Court of International Trade**, the **Court of Customs**, and the **Court of Military Appeals**.

3.2.4   The Federal Bureaucracy

In addition to the President's Cabinet and the Executive Office, a series of independent agencies makes up the federal bureaucracy, the so-called "**fourth branch**" of the national government. Most of these agencies were established to protect consumers and to regulate industries engaged in interstate trade. Others were set up to oversee government programs. From the time of the establishment of the Interstate Commerce Commission in 1887 these departments grew in number and influence. Late in the 1970s, the trend began to reverse, as some agencies were cut back and others eliminated altogether.

Among the most important of these powerful agencies are the **regulatory commissions**. The President appoints their administrators with the approval of the Senate. Unlike Cabinet secretaries and other high appointees, they cannot be dismissed by the chief executive. This system protects the independent status of the agencies. Following are examples of some of the major regulatory agencies and their functions.

Agency	**Regulatory Functions**
Interstate Commerce Commission	Monitors surface transportation and some pipelines
Federal Reserve Board	Supervises the banking system, sets interest rates, and controls the money supply
Federal Trade Commission	Protects consumers by looking into false advertising and antitrust violations
Federal Communications Commission	Polices the airwaves by licensing radio and television stations and regulating cable and telephone companies
Securities and Exchange Commission	Protects investors by monitoring the sale of stocks and bonds
National Labor Relations Board	Oversees labor and management practices

| Consumer Product Safety Commission | Sets standards of safety for manufactured products |
| Nuclear Regulatory Commission | Licenses and inspects nuclear power plants |

Another category of the "fourth branch" of government is made up of the **independent executive agencies**. These were created by Congress and resemble Cabinet departments, but they do not enjoy Cabinet status. Nonetheless they are powerful entities. Some of the key executive agencies include the Civil Rights Commission, the Environmental Protection Agency, and the National Aeronautics and Space Administration. Their names are indicative of their functions. The top level executives of these agencies are appointed by the President with the approval of the Senate.

Some of the independent agencies are actually **government corporations**. These are commercial enterprises created by Congress to perform a variety of necessary services. Their roots can be traced back to the **First Bank of the United States,** established in 1791 by Secretary of the Treasury **Alexander Hamilton**. The **Federal Deposit Insurance Corporation** (FDIC), which insures bank deposits, is a more recent example. Under **Franklin Roosevelt's New Deal**, the **Tennessee Valley Authority** (TVA) was authorized to revive a depressed region of the nation. Today it oversees the generation of electric power throughout a vast region and maintains flood control programs as well. The largest of the government corporations and the most familiar to the general public is the **United States Postal Service**. The original Post Office Department was established in 1775 by the Second Continental Congress, and it enjoyed Cabinet status. It was reorganized in 1970 in hopes that it would eventually become self-supporting.

The large and powerful federal bureaucracy shapes and administers government policy. It is inherently political despite sporadic efforts throughout the years to maintain the integrity of the bureaucratic staff. Dating back to the administrations of **Andrew Jackson**, the practice of handing out government jobs in return for political favors (**spoils system**) had been the rule. The **Civil Service Act** (the

Pendleton Act) was passed in 1883 in an attempt to reform the spoils system. Federal workers were to be recruited on the basis of merit determined by a competitive examination. Veterans were given preferential status. The Civil Service system was reorganized in the 1970s with the creation of the **Office of Personnel Management**. The OPM is charged with recruiting, training, and promoting government workers. Merit is the stated objective when hiring federal employees. A controversial policy of the OPM is affirmative action, a program to help groups discriminated against in the job market to find employment.

3.3 Political Beliefs and Characteristics of Citizens

The population of the United States, with its diverse components, is difficult to characterize with respect to political beliefs and attitudes. The process by which individuals form their political allegiances is called **political socialization**. Several factors (**cleavages**) are relevant to the formation of political opinions including family, race, gender, class, religion, education, and region. Following are some generalizations as to the impact of these cleavages on an individual's political identification and activity.

Family – affiliation with a political party is commonly passed from one generation to another.

Race – African Americans tend to be more liberal than whites on economic, social, and public policy issues.

Gender – women tend to be more liberal than men.

Class – citizens from the middle and upper classes tend to be more politically active than those from the lower socioeconomic brackets. Low income voters tend to identify more with the liberal agenda.

Religion – Protestants tend to be more conservative than Catholics and Jews. Evangelical Protestants seem to be most conservative on ethical and moral issues.

Education – higher education seems to have a liberalizing effect that remains potent after schooling is completed.

Region – Southerners tend to be most conservative, mid-westerners more liberal, and those living on the East and West coasts the most liberal of all.

Despite the categorization of Americans as either **liberals** or **conservatives,** most studies indicate that they do not follow clearly delineated **ideologies** (firm and consistent beliefs with respect to political, economic, and social issues). The terms liberal and conservative with reference to the political beliefs of Americans are difficult to define in precise terms. Liberals tend to favor change and to view government as a tool for improving the quality of life. Conservatives, on the other hand, are more inclined to view both change and government with suspicion. They emphasize individual initiative and local solutions to problems. A puzzling reversal is seen in the attitudes of liberals and conservatives when confronting moral issues such as abortion and school prayer. Here conservatives see a role for government in ensuring the moral climate of the nation while liberals stress the importance of individual choice.

3.4 Political Institutions and Special Interests

Civic culture in the United States is dominated by the two major political parties and is heavily influenced by the activities of interest groups and the mass media. These latter forces, both directly and indirectly, are largely responsible for molding and swaying public opinion.

3.4.1 Political Parties

A **political party** is an organization that seeks to influence government by electing candidates to public office. The party provides a label for candidates, recruits and campaigns, and tries to organize and control the legislative and executive branches of government through a set of leaders.

The Constitution does not mention political parties, and the Founders in general were opposed to them. Yet they developed simultaneously with the organization of the new government in 1789. It was the initial conflict over the interpretation of the powers assigned to the new government by the Constitution that gave rise to the first organized American political parties.

The **Federalist Party** evolved around the policies of Washington's Secretary of the Treasury, **Alexander Hamilton**. He and his supporters favored a "**loose construction**" approach to the interpretation of the Constitution. They advocated a strong federal government with the power to assume any duties and responsibilities not prohibited to it by the text of the document. They generally supported programs designed to benefit banking and commercial interests, and in foreign policy, the Federalists were **pro-British**.

The **Democratic** or **Jeffersonian Republicans** formed in opposition to the Federalists. They rallied around Washington's Secretary of State, **Thomas Jefferson**. The Jeffersonians took a "**strict constructionist**" approach, interpreting the Constitution in a narrow, limited sense. Sympathetic to the needs of the "common man," the Democratic-Republicans were mistrustful of powerful centralized government. They saw the small farmers, shopkeepers, and laborers as the backbone of the nation. In the area of foreign affairs, the Democratic-Republicans were **pro-French**. The present day Democratic Party traces its roots to the Jeffersonians.

By the 1820s, the Democrats had splintered into factions led by **Andrew Jackson** (the Democrats) and **John Quincy Adams** (National Republicans). The Jacksonians continued with Jefferson's tradition of supporting policies designed to enhance the power of the common man. Their support was largely agrarian. The National Republicans, like their Federalist predecessors, represented the interests of bankers, merchants, and some large planters. Eventually a new party, the **Whigs**, was organized from the remnants of the old Federalists and the National Republicans. The Whigs were prominent during the 1840s, but like their Democratic rivals, they fragmented during the 1850s over the divisive slavery issue. The modern **Republican Party** was born in 1854 as Whigs and anti-slavery Democrats came together to halt the spread of slavery. The Republicans built a constituency around the interests of business, farmers, workers, and the newly emancipated slaves in the post-Civil War era.

Political parties exert a variety of functions essential to the democratic tradition in the United States. Nominating candidates, local, state, and national office is their most visible activity. At the national level, this function has been diluted somewhat by the popularity of **primary elections** allowing voters to express their preference for candidates. Raucous conventions where party bosses chose obscure **"dark horse"** candidates in "smoke filled rooms" are largely a thing of the past.

Political parties stimulate interest in public issues by highlighting their own strengths and maximizing the flaws of the opposition. They also provide a framework for keeping the machinery of government operating, most notably in their control of Congress and its organization, which is strictly along party lines.

American political parties appear in theory to be highly organized. The geographic size of the country coupled with the federal system of government keep the parties in a state of relative decentralization. At the local level, the fundamental unit of organization is the **precinct**. At this level, there is usually a captain or committee to handle such routine chores as registering voters, distributing party literature, organizing **"grass-roots"** meetings, and getting out the vote on election day.

State central committees are critical to the parties' fund raising activities. They also organize the state party conventions. There is great variety from state to state regarding the composition and selection of the state committees, which often formulate policies independent from those of the national committee.

In presidential election years, the **national party committees** are most visible. They plan the **national nominating convention**, write the party **platforms** (summaries of positions on major issues), raise money to finance political activities, and carry out the election campaigns. Representatives from each state serve on the national committees, and the **presidential nominee** chooses the individual to serve as the **party chairperson**.

Although the two-party system is firmly established in the United States, over the years, **"third parties"** have left their marks. The national nominating conventions were introduced in the 1830s by the **Anti-Masonic Party** and were soon adopted by the Democrats and the Whigs. The **Prohibition Party** opposed the use of alcohol and worked for the adoption of the **Eighteenth Amendment**. In the 1890s, the **Populist Party** championed the causes of the farmers and workers and impacted the mainstream parties with its reform agenda. Among the Populist innovations were the **initiative petition** (a mechanism allowing voters to put proposed legislation on the ballot) and the **referendum** (allows voters to approve or reject laws passed by their legislatures). The **Progressive** or **Bull Moose Party** was a **splinter party** (one that breaks away from an established party, in this case the Republican Party) built around the personality of Theodore Roosevelt. Another party formed around the personality of a forceful individual was the 1992 **Independent Party** of **H. Ross Perot**. Perot did not capture any electoral votes but garnered nineteen percent of the popular tally.

3.4.2 Elections

In comparison to citizens in other democratic systems, Americans elect a large number of public officials. Elections in the United States are largely regulated by **state** law. The Constitution does assign to Congress the responsibility for determining "the times, places, and manner of holding elections for Senators and Representatives." Article II establishes the Electoral College for presidential elections and specifies that they shall be held on the same day throughout the nation. Several of the Amendments deal with election procedures, voter qualifications, and **suffrage** (the right to vote) for target groups (former slaves, women, and those eighteen years of age and older). Nonetheless, the principal responsibility for arranging and supervising elections rests with the states.

The actual election process consists of two phases: nominating the candidates and choosing the final officials. **Primary elections** screen and select the final party candidates. **Closed primaries** allow voters **registered** (legal procedure that must be completed before an individual can vote) in one of the political parties to express their preferences for the final candidate from among the field of hopefuls in that party. **Open primaries** allow voters to select their party affiliations on site. Some states allow "**crossover**" voting which permits voters registered in one party to vote for candidates in the other party. This practice can lead to the tactic of voting for the weakest choice in the opposition party to give an advantage in the final election to the candidate and the party the voter actually supports.

In **national elections** (those held in November of each even-numbered year to choose national officeholders), the **campaign** traditionally begins after Labor Day. **Off-year elections** are those in which only members of Congress are chosen and no presidential contest is held. In both presidential and off-year elections, candidates follow exhausting schedules and spend huge sums on media advertising. Their activities usually dominate the national and local news coverage, and debates are common forums for airing their differences. Funding for political campaigns comes from a variety of sources including the candidates own resources, private supporters, **Political Action Committees** (PACs), and the federal government. In the election reform drive of the 1970s, the **Federal Election Commission** was created to ensure that laws concerning campaign financing are followed.

The cost of the elections themselves is borne by the state and local governments which must prepare ballots, designate polling places, and pay workers who participate in administering the elections. **Registrars of voters** oversee the preparation of ballots, the establishment of polling places, and the tallying of the votes. In a close election, the loser may request a **recount**. Some states require them in closely contested races.

3.4.3 Voter Behavior

In recent years, attention has focused on the problem of voter apathy. Despite efforts to extend suffrage to all segments of the adult population, participation in the electoral process has been on the decline. Several theories have been advanced to explain this trend. There is widespread belief that Americans are dissatisfied with their government and mistrust all elected officials. Therefore, they refuse

37

to participate in the electoral process. Some citizens do not vote in a given election, not because they are "turned-off" to the system, but because they are ill, homeless, away on business, or otherwise preoccupied on election day. College students and others away from their legal residences find registration and the use of **absentee ballots** cumbersome and inconvenient. Efforts have been made in the 1990s to streamline the registration process with such legislation as the **"motor-voter" bill** that makes it possible for citizens to register at their local registries of motor vehicles.

While most attempts to explain voter apathy focus on negatives such as citizen apathy, some analysts disagree. They see disinterest in the ballot as a sign that the majority of Americans are happy with the system and feel no sense of urgency to participate in the political process.

Political participation is not limited to voting in elections. Working for candidates, attending rallies, contacting elected officials and sharing opinions about issues, writing letters to newspapers, marching in protest, and joining in community activities are all forms of political participation. While voter turnout has decreased in recent years, other forms of participation seem to be on the increase.

3.4.4   Interest Groups

American officials and political leaders are continually subjected to pressure from a variety of **interest groups** seeking to influence their actions. Such groups arise from bonds among individuals who share common concerns. Interest groups may be loosely organized (**informal**), with no clear structure or regulations. A good example of such an informal or ad hoc interest group was the "March of the Poor" on Washington, D.C., in 1963 to focus Congress's attention on the needs of the "underclass" in America. A group of neighbors united in opposition to a new shopping mall that threatens a wetland is an example of this type of group. Other interest groups are much more **formal** and permanent in nature. They may have suites of offices and large numbers of employees. Their political objectives are usually clearly defined. Labor unions, professional and public-interest groups, and single issue organizations fall into this category.

The National Rifle Association and the National Right to Life Organization are examples of **single issue** pressure groups.

Interest groups employ a variety of tactics to accomplish their goals. Most commonly, they **lobby** (influence the passage or defeat of legislation) elected officials, particularly members of Congress. Lobbyists provide legislators with reports and statistics to persuade them of the legitimacy of their respective positions. They may present expert testimony at public hearings and influence the media to portray their causes in a favorable light. Lobbyists are required to register in Washington and to make their positions public. They are barred from presenting false and misleading information and from bribing public officials. Regulatory legislation cannot, however, curb all the abuses inherent to a system of organized persuasion.

One particularly controversial brand of pressure group is the **Political Action Committee** (PAC). PACs were formed in the 1970s in an attempt to circumvent legislation limiting contributions to political campaigns. Critics see these interest groups as another means of diluting the influence individual voters may have on their elected officials. Some politicians refuse to accept PAC money.

3.4.5 Public Opinion

Public opinion refers to the attitudes and preferences expressed by a significant number of individuals about an issue that involves the government or the society at large. It does not necessarily represent the sentiments of all or even most of the citizenry. Nonetheless, it is an important component of a democratic society.

In today's technological society, the influence of the **mass media** on public opinion cannot be overemphasized. The print and broadcast media can reach large numbers of people cheaply and efficiently, but the electronic media in particular have been criticized for oversimplifying complicated issues and reducing coverage of major events to brief sound bites. Both the print and broadcast media claim to present news in a fair and objective format, but both conservatives and liberals claim that coverage is slanted. **Paid political advertising** is another vehicle for molding public opinion. In this case, objectivity is neither expected nor attempted, as candidates and interest groups employ "hard-sell" techniques to persuade voters to support their causes.

Measuring the effects of the media on public opinion is difficult, as is gauging where the public stands on a given issue at a particular point in time. **Public opinion polls** have been designed to these ends. Pollsters usually address a **random sample** and try to capture a **cross-section** of the population. Their questions are designed to elicit responses that do not mirror the biases of the interviewer or the polling organization. Results are tabulated and analyzed, and generalizations are presented to the media.

Although polls are more accurate today than in the past, they are still subject to criticism for oversimplifying complicated issues and encouraging pat answers to complex problems. Public opinion is constantly in a state of flux, and what may be a valid report today is tomorrow passé. Another criticism is that interviewees may not be entirely candid, particularly with respect to sensitive issues. They may answer as they think they should but not necessarily with full honesty.

A type of election poll that has been the target of sharp criticism is the **exit poll** in which interviewers question subjects about their votes as they leave the polling places. These polls may be accurate, but if the media present the results while voting is still in progress, the outcome may be affected. Predicting the winners before voters throughout the country have had the opportunity to cast their ballots in a national election robs a segment of the electorate of the sense that its participation is of any consequence. In recent presidential elections, broadcast outlets have shown more sensitivity to this problem.

3.5   Civil Rights and Individual Liberties

Civil rights are those legal claims that individuals have to protect themselves from discrimination at the hands of both the government and other citizens. They include the right to vote, equality before the law, and access to public facilities. **Individual** or **civil liberties** protect the sanctity of the person from arbitrary governmental interference. In this category belong the fundamental freedoms of speech, religion, press, and rights such as **due process**

(government must act fairly and follow established procedures, as in legal proceedings).

The origin of the concept of fundamental rights and freedoms can be traced to the British constitutional heritage and to the theorists of the Enlightenment. Jefferson's **Declaration of Independence** contains several references to the crown's failure to uphold the civil rights that British subjects had come to value and expect. When fashioning the Constitution, the Founding Fathers included passages regarding the protection of civil liberties, such as the provision in Article I for maintaining the right of *habeas corpus*. One of the criticisms of the Constitution lodged by its opponents was that it did not go far enough in safeguarding individual rights. During the first session of Congress in 1789, the first ten amendments (the **Bill of Rights**) were adopted and sent to the states for ratification. These amendments contain many of the protections that define the ideals of American life. The Bill of Rights was meant to limit the power of the federal government to restrict the freedom of individual citizens. The **Fourteenth Amendment** of 1868 prohibits **states** from denying civil rights and individual liberties to their residents. The Supreme Court is charged with interpreting the law, particularly as it applies to civil rights and individual liberties cases. Not until the **Gitlow Case** in 1925 did the Supreme Court begin to exercise this function with respect to state enforcement of the Bill of Rights. States are now expected to conform to the federal standard of civil rights.

The Amendment that is most closely identified with individual liberty in the United States is the **First Amendment**, which protects freedom of religion, speech, press, assembly, and petition. The First Amendment sets forth the principle of **separation of Church and State** with its "**free exercise**" and "**establishment**" clauses. These have led the Supreme Court to rule against such practices as school prayer (**Engle v. Vitale 1962**) and Bible reading in public schools (**Abington Township v. Schempp 1963**).

The **Fourth Amendment**, which outlawed "**unreasonable searches and seizures**," mandates that warrants be granted only "**upon probable cause**," and affirms the "**right of the people to be secure in their persons**," is fundamental to the Court's interpretation of due process and the rights of the accused. The **Fifth Amendment**, which calls for a grand jury, outlawed **double jeopardy** (trying a person who has been acquitted of a charge for a second time) and states that a person may not be compelled to be a witness against himself, is also the basis for Supreme Court rulings that protect the accused. "**Cruel and unusual punishments**" are banned by the **Eighth Amendment**. This clause has been invoked by opponents of capital punishment to justify their position, but the Supreme Court has ruled that the death penalty can be applied if states are judicious and use equal standards in sentencing those convicted of capital crimes to death.

In the twentieth century, a major concern for litigation and review by the Supreme Court has been in the area of civil rights for minorities, particularly African Americans. When civil rights organizations such as the NAACP brought a series of cases before the courts under the "**equal protection clause**" of the **Fourteenth Amendment**, they began to enjoy some victories. Earlier when the Supreme Court enforced its "**separate but equal**" doctrine in the 1896 **Plessy v. Ferguson Case**, it did not apply the equal protection standard and allowed segregation to be maintained. The Court reversed itself in 1954 in the landmark case, **Brown v. Board of Education**, which ruled that separate but equal was unconstitutional. This ruling led to an end to most **de jure** (legally enforced) segregation, but **de facto** (exists in fact) segregation persisted, largely due to housing patterns and racial and ethnic enclaves in urban neighborhoods.

3.5.1 Landmark Supreme Court Cases

In addition to the previously cited Supreme Court rulings in civil rights and individual liberties cases, the following landmark decisions are notable for their relevance to the concepts of civil rights and individual freedoms.

- **Dred Scott v. Sanford** (1857) – ruled that as a slave Scott had no right to sue for his freedom, and further that Congressional prohibitions against slavery in U.S. territories were unlawful.

- **Near v. Minnesota** (1931) – states were barred from using the concept of prior restraint (outlawing something before it has taken place) to discourage the publication of objectionable material except during wartime or in the cases of obscenity or incitement to violence.

- **West Virginia Board of Education v. Barnette** (1943) – overturned an earlier decision and ruled that compulsory saluting of the flag was unconstitutional.

- **Korematsu v. United States** (1944) – upheld the legality of the forced evacuation of persons of Japanese ancestry during World War II as a wartime necessity.

- **Mapp v. Ohio** (1961) – extended the Supreme Court's exclusionary rule, which bars at trial the introduction of evidence that has not been legally obtained to states. The Court has modified this ruling, particularly with reference to drug cases, so that evidence that might not initially have been obtained legally, but which would eventually have turned up in lawful procedures, can be introduced.

- **Gideon v. Wainwright** (1963) – ruled that courts must provide legal counsel to poor defendants in all felony cases. A later ruling extended this right to all defendants facing possible prison sentences.

- **Escobedo v. Illinois** (1964) – extended the right to counsel to include consultation prior to interrogation by authorities.

- **Miranda v. Arizona** (1966) – mandated that all suspects be informed of their due process rights before questioning by police.

- **Tinker v. Des Moines School District** (1969) – defined the wearing of black armbands in school in protest against the Vietnam War as "symbolic speech" protected by the First Amendment.

- **New York Times v. United States** (1971) – allowed, under the First Amendment's freedom of the press protection, the publication of the controversial Pentagon Papers during the Vietnam War.

- **Roe v. Wade** (1973) – legalized abortion so long as a fetus is not viable (able to survive outside the womb).

- **Bakke v. Regents of the University of California** (1978) – declared the University's quota system to be unconstitutional while upholding the legitimacy of affirmative action policies in which institutions consider race and gender as factors when determining admissions.

- **Hazelwood School District v. Kuhlmeier** (1988) – ruled that freedom of the press does not extend to student publications that might be construed as sponsored by the school.

CHAPTER 4

Comparative Government and Politics

This subfield of government and politics includes two principal areas of scholarship and information: the theoretical frameworks for the government structures, functions, and political cultures of nations and a comparative analysis of the political systems of a series of targeted nations or societies.

4.1 Theoretical Frameworks for Government Structures, Functions, and Political Culture

4.1.1 Environmental Factors

In order to understand the political institutions and civic life of any nation, several environmental factors need to be considered. Such questions as the **size, location, geographic features, economic strength, level of industrialization** and **cultural diversity** of a society must be explored. Both the **domestic** and **international** contexts need to be examined as well as the level of **dependence** on or **independence** from the world community. The location of the United States in the Western Hemisphere, separated from both Europe and Asia by vast expanses of ocean, is a critical component in the development of its relatively independent political culture. Conversely the location of Eastern European countries in the shadow of the post World War II Soviet Union led to political dependence. The cultural diversity and traditional hostilities of the Balkan peoples are key elements in the political and military volatility of the region. Industrialization and economic stability are conditions that are commonly conducive to a highly developed political system.

The **age** and **historical traditions** of a nation have great impact on its current political culture. France's contemporary unitary form of government can be viewed as an evolutionary manifestation of earlier traditions that centralized power in divine right monarchs and ambitious emperors. **Legitimacy** (acceptance by citizens) is quite another prospect in such places as Somalia and Haiti with their unstable political histories and economic vulnerability.

4.1.2 Government Structures and Functions

How a government is organized, its mechanisms for carrying out its mission, the scope of that mission, and how its structures and functions compare with other governments are prime considerations in comparative government.

The **geographic distribution of authority and responsibility** is a key variable. **Confederations**, such as the United States under the Articles of Confederation, have weak central governments and delegate principal authority to smaller units such as the states. **Federal systems**, on the other hand, divide sovereignty between a central government and those of their separate states. Brazil, India, and the United States are contemporary examples of federal republics. Highly centralized, **unitary** forms of government concentrate power and authority at the top, as in France and Japan.

Separation of governmental powers is another aspect of structure useful in comparing political systems. **Authoritarian** governments center power in a single or collective executive, with the legislative and judicial bodies having little input. The former Soviet Union is an example. Great Britain typifies the **parliamentary** form of government. Here legislative and executive combine, with a prime minister and cabinet selected from within the legislative body. They maintain power only so long as the legislative assembly supports their major policies. The **democratic presidential** system of the United States clearly separates the legislative, executive, and judicial structures. The branches, particularly the executive and the legislative, must cooperate, however, in order for policy to be consistent and for government operations to be carried out smoothly.

A third aspect of governmental structure and function involves the **limits** placed on the power to govern. This facet of politics closely reflects the theoretical and ideological roots of a system. **Constitutional** systems limit the powers of government through written and/ or unwritten sources. Law, custom, and precedent combine to protect individuals from the unchecked power of a central authority. The United States and Great Britain have constitutional governments. **Authoritarian** regimes, such as those found in China and the former Soviet Union, do not limit the power of the central authority over the lives of individuals. Those in control impose their values and their will on the society at large regardless of popular sentiments. Authoritarianism is associated with **Fascism, Nazism,** and **totalitarianism** in general.

4.1.3 Political Culture, Parties, Participation, and Mechanisms for Change

Understanding a nation's **political culture** is key to analyzing the theoretical foundations, structure, and functions of its government. It can be defined as the aggregate values a society shares about how politics and government should operate. Some societies function from a **consensus** framework, while other political cultures are more **conflicted**. The Soviet Union's political culture after World War II, as contrasted with the situation there in the early 1990s, illustrates the difference between consensual and conflicted societies. The vehicles for transmitting the political culture and the social cleavages that characterize that culture will impact its system of governing and its legitimacy in the minds of its citizenry. Analysis of the extent to which citizens support their political systems is an important component of comparative government.

Questions regarding the methods citizens employ to impact their political systems and the ease of their access to the power structure need to be examined. Do elections offer a **choice** between candidates with diverse programs and contrasting agendas, as is often the case in the United States, or do they present citizens the opportunity to show their support for the government in a **one party** system such as in China? The number, nature, and power of political parties are additional factors for analysis with respect to how the demands and concerns of citizens in various nations are represented and met. The presence and proliferation of other interest groups such as labor unions and environmental activists provide additional clues as to the values and methods of a political culture.

Beyond voting in elections and joining and supporting political parties and interest groups, **citizen participation** can take other forms. Contacting politicians, lobbying for legislation, and demonstrating in the streets are common vehicles for involvement in the political life of a nation. The degree to which such expressions are encouraged and tolerated by government officials is another facet of political culture that varies from society to society.

Comparative politics and government as a field is concerned with **mechanisms for change** in different nations. Can citizens effect reform through ballots, protest, public opinion polls, or revolts? The underlying factors precipitating the need for change are relevant to an understanding of the overall process.

4.2 Government and Politics in the United Kingdom (Britain)

4.2.1 Geographic and Historical Context

The political unit of the United Kingdom (UK) is made up of England, Scotland, Wales (Great Britain), and Northern Ireland. Both geography and history have played significant roles in shaping the political life of the nation. Traditionally a major player in European and international politics, Britain is, at the same time, insulated by the English Channel and the North Sea and able to distance itself from the affairs of the continent. Facilitated by a powerful navy, the British embarked on an aggressive policy of imperialism in the seventeenth and eighteenth centuries and built a formidable empire. The empire, coupled with the industrialization of the eighteenth and nineteenth centuries, contributed to Britain's power and independence. A contemporary example of Britain's aloofness from the rest of Western Europe is its tardiness in joining the European Community (EC), which did not materialize until 1973.

Britain has one of the oldest constitutional governments in the world. While political stability and representative government are defining characteristics of British life, cultural diversity has contributed to tension and internal unrest. The people of England, Scotland, Wales, and Northern Ireland preserve their distinct cultural identities, and the latter has been torn apart by religious conflict for decades. Recently voices have been raised in Scotland in support of greater autonomy. The post World War II decline of the British empire coupled with economic stagnation have taken their toll on Britain's stature as a world power.

4.2.2 Government Structures and Functions

Britain's **constitution** is unique in that, unlike its American counterpart, which is a single written document, it is largely **unwritten** and relies heavily on **tradition** and **precedent**. It consists of the following components:

- **Historical documents** such as the **Magna Carta** (1215), which forced the king to cede some of his power to the nobility and the 1689 **Bill of Rights**, an affirmation of the supremacy of Parliament over the crown.

- Landmark **acts of Parliament** such as the **Reform Act of 1832**, which enfranchised England's middle class, and the **Parliament Acts of 1911 and 1949**, bills that greatly diminished the power of the **House of Lords**.

- English **common law** and **judicial precedent**.

- British **conventions**, such as the annual meetings of Parliament and the selection of the prime minister from the ranks of the House of Commons.

Like the United States Constitution, the British model is flexible enough to adapt to changing conditions. Both **parliamentary statutes** and **common law precedents** serve to "amend" the British constitution.

As a **constitutional monarchy**, the United Kingdom has a hereditary **head of state**, whose duties and responsibilities are primarily ceremonial. The British monarch has the right to both convene and dissolve Parliament, to accept the resignations of prime ministers and cabinets that have lost the support of the majority in Parliament, and to invite the head of the majority party in the House of Commons to form a new government. The monarch goes through the formality of giving assent to bills passed by Parliament. A key function of the British monarch is to stand as a symbol of the nation and to provide a sense of tradition and continuity.

The true **executive** power in Britain resides in the Prime Minister and the Cabinet. Unlike the system in the United States, which separates the executive and legislative branches, in the United Kingdom, the executives are members of legislature. Since 1902, the Prime Minister has been selected from the majority party in the House of Commons where he/she is regarded as "first among equals." Together with the Cabinet, the Prime Minister must design and carry out a party program that receives the support of the majority in the House of Commons. **Elections** to the House of Commons are held every **five years** or sooner if the Prime Minister and the cabinet lose the confidence of the majority.

The **legislature** of Britain is **bicameral**, consisting of an upper house (**House of Lords**) and a lower house (**House of Commons**). The House of Lords is the secondary chamber, today serving principally as an advisory body. Members are either **hereditary** or **honorary** (life peers). The latter cannot transfer their membership to their offspring. The center of the government in Britain is the **House of Commons**. Its membership (650 in 1995) is popularly elected from single-member districts or **parliamentary boroughs**. The controlling majority is charged with passage of the legislation that is drafted by the Cabinet. It can force an election by a **vote of no confidence** in the policies of the Prime Minister and the Cabinet. **Party discipline** is tight, and the **party line** on legislation is officially communicated in regular memos issued by the party leadership. An important function of the House of Commons is to groom potential prime ministers and cabinet members, since they are all selected from within the ranks of the legislature.

4.2.3   Political Culture, Parties, and Participation

British political culture is characterized by **stability** in government that dates back to the Seventeenth Century's Glorious Revolution when, in return for the crown, William and Mary acceded to the restrictions placed on them by the Parliament. Another factor characteristic of the British political system is the long tradition of civil authority having precedence over religious authority in matters of state. The **supremacy of state over church** was established in the 1500s when Henry VIII severed his ties with the Pope and named himself head of the Church of England. Later as Britain industrialized, the educational system was improved creating a greater demand for enfranchisement of the burgeoning middle class. The Labour Party's birth in 1900 provided the industrial class with a powerful voice in Parliament. The House of Lords declined in influence, but it didn't disappear. The same is true for the monarchy. These attempts to preserve traditions while at the same time adapting the institutions of government to changing conditions, through measures such as the creation of the welfare state to provide essential services to citizens, have gone far toward maintaining a stable political climate.

The political party is an essential component of British politics. The House of Commons is organized on party lines, and it is the responsibility of the parties to groom candidates, conduct elections, and formulate the legislative agenda. While a multi-party structure exists in Britain, the competitive **two-party system** has historically dominated parliament. Currently the **Conservative** and **Labour** Parties prevail, but there are signs that regional parties in Scotland, Wales, and Northern Ireland may become more important in the future. Challenges have also come from the Social Democratic Party and the Liberal Alliance. The ideological differences between the two principal parties focus on economic questions with the Labour Party favoring the nationalization of major industries and government intervention to reduce disparities in wealth. The Conservatives are identified with free market economics, nationalistic foreign policy, and traditional social and moral values. Since the 1970s, the lines separating membership in the British Conservative and Labour Parties have blurred somewhat with more working class voters supporting the Conservatives and more middle class voters aligned with the Labour Party than in earlier decades. Economic decline in the United Kingdom in the 1970s led to a rejection of the Labour program and increased support for the Conservatives. Conservatives Margaret Thatcher and John Major dominated British politics in the 1980s and 1990s.

The single-member district, **winner-take-all** (either by a majority or plurality) electoral system in Britain greatly favors the perpetuation of the power of the two major parties. A single party candidate represents each of the parliamentary boroughs. There is no mechanism for proportional representation based on the percentage of support each party may receive in a given election. This situation makes it difficult for minor parties to gain representation in Parliament.

Despite a heavy emphasis on traditions and the challenges facing its minor political parties, the British constitutional system allows for gradual change and adaptation to new conditions. The five year rule for general parliamentary elections and the system of earlier elections if the Prime Minister and the Cabinet lose the confidence of the majority in the House of Commons are mechanisms for orderly expression of discontent and fresh leadership. Economic problems and a loss of pre-eminence in the international theater have not tarnished significantly the United Kingdom's image as a model of stable constitutional government responsive to public opinion and respectful of the rights of individual citizens.

4.3 Government and Politics in France

4.3.1 Geographic and Historical Context

Relatively large in size geographically (about 20% smaller than the state of Texas), France's unique location places it on the Atlantic while at the same time anchoring it to both continental Europe and the Mediterranean. Sharing borders with a number of European neighbors, France has necessarily been deeply involved in international affairs throughout its turbulent history. Economically, France is both industrialized and agricultural, with the pre-eminence of its capital city of Paris at times enhanced at the expense of the outer provinces and smaller urban centers.

At present, France is governed by the constitution of the **Fifth Republic**, which retains some significant aspects of both its absolutist past and the republican spirit of the French Revolution. Prior to the overthrow of the Bourbon dynasty in 1789, French monarchs ruled by **divine right** and enjoyed absolute power. Louis XIV's famous dictum *"L'état c'est moi"* (**I am the state**) is an accurate reflection of the nature of sovereignty under the old regime. The French Revolution radically altered this concept of governing with its founding documents (Declaration of the Rights of Man and a constitution) based on American models and its slogan, "**liberty, equality, fraternity.**" The First Republic's innovations such as the **National Assembly** and the use of the **plebiscite** (popular referendum to endorse government policy) were retained when Napoleon Bonaparte seized power in the chaos of the revolutionary era. However, he ruled with the absolutist power that had characterized the Bourbon monarchy.

After a long period of instability, the **Third Republic** was established in 1870. It prevailed until WWII when the German occupation began. In 1944, the charismatic leader of the Free French resistance movement, **Charles de Gaulle**, created the short-lived **Fourth Republic**. He resigned in 1946 after a trend toward party rule that diminished the role of the President. In 1958 after a humiliating defeat in southeast Asia and in the midst of the War for Algerian Independence, de Gaulle was invited to form a new government. The **Fifth Republic**, a mixed presidential-parliamentary system, was created under a unique constitution that reflects France's blended heritage of both absolutist and republican strands.

4.3.2 Government Structures and Functions

The constitution of the **Fifth Republic** designates the bulk of power to the **President**, the chief of state. Theoretically, the President shares executive power with the Prime Minister. However, under the French **"dual executive"** system, it is the President who is the dominant political figure. The President is elected by popular vote for a term of seven years. He/she can be re-elected an unlimited number of times. The President appoints the Prime Minister as well as the members of the **Council of Ministers** (Cabinet). The Prime Minister is typically chosen from the majority party or coalition and consequently serves as a liaison between the President and the National Assembly. The Prime Minister's principal task is to oversee the operation of the government, but it is the President who is the acknowledged leader. The President is charged with protecting the constitution and with guaranteeing both the independence and the territorial integrity of the nation. The President may appeal for popular support through the use of the plebiscite and may dissolve the Parliament and call for new elections. In addition, he/she is also the **commander-in-chief**, has the power to negotiate and ratify treaties, and may issue decrees to deal with emergency situations. Clearly the "**de Gaulle Constitution**" of the Fifth Republic, an appeal to the former glory and greatness of France, bestows on the President an array of powers unusual in a parliamentary republic.

The **Cabinet** directs the policy-making functions of government. Its members plan legislation, direct the activities of the houses of the Parliament, and can require that their favored proposals receive priority treatment.

The French **Parliament** is **bicameral**, consisting of the **National Assembly** and the **Senate**. The members of the National Assembly are elected for five year terms by universal suffrage. The Assembly meets for an annual six-month session and may be dissolved by the President (no more than twice a year). While the National Assembly cannot set its own agenda, it is constitutionally legitimate for it to develop legislation in certain areas such as civil rights, nationalization of industry, and electoral procedures. The Senate is elected indirectly by means of an electoral college. Senators serve nine year terms and disproportionately represent the rural areas of France. The government is not accountable to the Senate, which can be easily bypassed in the legislative procedure when the National Assembly is asked to pass a bill by a simple majority.

RELATIONSHIP BETWEEN FRENCH
LEGISLATIVE AND EXECUTIVE BRANCHES

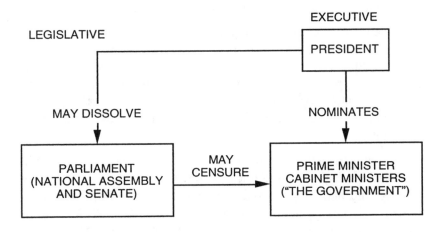

The **judicial** arm of the national government is the **Constitutional Council**. It is comprised of nine judges who serve terms of nine years' duration. One third are selected by the President, one third by the President of the National Assembly, and one third by the President of the Senate. All past presidents of the Republic are members *ex-officio*. The Constitutional Council exercises the power of judicial review with respect to the constitutionality of the laws and oversees election procedures. In addition it must be consulted before the President can issue emergency decrees.

4.3.3 Political Culture, Parties, and Participation

The political culture of France clearly reflects its conflicted historical tradition. The Fifth Republic's emphasis on presidential power can be traced to the legacy of the Bourbon monarchs and powerful rulers such as Napoleon Bonaparte, Louis Napoleon, and Charles de Gaulle. On the other hand, the republican tradition, born in the French Revolution, stresses the importance of representation and the National Assembly. The frequent use of the plebiscite seemingly circumvents both the executive and legislative branches, yet it has been a tool of powerful rulers to rubber stamp executive policies. These contradictions coupled with France's unsettled past have produced a distrust of politics among the population at large and a widespread belief that only major upheavals will produce significant change.

The government of contemporary France operates under a multiparty system that makes single-party domination of the Parliament difficult. Philosophically and pragmatically, France's political parties span a wide political spectrum from **Left** to **Right**. These designations originated during the French Revolution when radicals were seated on the left side of the General Assembly and conservatives on the right.

In comparison to other representative democracies such as Britain, the French allegiance to political parties tends to be weak with low membership and frequent switches. Parties tend to be narrowly focused, with those on the Left more ideological and those on the Right more inclined to identify with a charismatic personality. Majorities in Parliament often depend on tentative **coalitions** (temporary alliances), a situation that contributes to instability in the government overall. During the weak Fourth Republic, governments toppled with alarming regularity. The situation has been more stable during the Fifth Republic but tends to be dependent upon the effectiveness of a strong president. Current French political parties include the following:

Parties on the Left

- **The Communist Party (PC)**, which was affiliated with the Soviet Union until its demise in the early 1990s, is supported by industrial workers and espouses radical programs.

- **The Socialist Party (PS)** resembles the British Labour Party in its support of welfare state programs. It was revived in the 1970s under the leadership of François Mitterrand and attracted support from civil servants and professionals not usually drawn to socialist policies.

Parties on the Right

- **The Union for French Democracy (UDF)** is a centrist coalition of groups that broke away from the more conservative Gaullist Party, protesting the latter's overuse of the plebiscite. Its most important leader was Giscard d'Estiang, who served as President from 1974–1981. The urban middle class forms the core of its support.

- **The Rally for the Republic (RPR)** is the neo-Gaullist party. Originally the Gaullists crystallized around the conservative, patriotic policies of their leader. Residents of rural France as well as members of the middle and upper classes tend to support the Gaullists. This party surged in power during the 1960s under the organizational direction of de Gaulle's prime minister, Georges Pompidou, who assumed the presidency when the former retired. The Gaullists suffered a sharp decline after de Gaulle's tenure, but they have been rejuvenated by Jacques Chirac, who became President in 1995.

- **The National Front (FN)**, a very conservative group, supports free market economics and nationalistic policies. The National Front is firmly opposed to immigration and international cooperation.

In addition to the major parties, smaller groups exist that bridge the gaps between the principal political organizations. Some represent extreme positions, and others resemble interest groups more than they do political parties. They may focus on single issues and cut across traditional party lines. Examples of such groups include environmentalists and activists for women's rights.

4.4 Government and Politics in the Former Soviet Union (Russia and the Commonwealth of Independent States)

4.4.1 Geographic and Historical Context

A vast territory spanning the upper regions of both Europe and Asia, the former Soviet Union is and has always been greatly impacted by its geography. Both Russian and later Soviet governments largely determined policy with geographic considerations in mind. In the Fifteenth Century, the princes of Moscow, a harsh, landlocked area in the northeast, expanded their holdings, and future rulers sought access to warm ocean ports. **Peter the Great**, czar in the later Seventeenth and early Eighteenth Centuries, established the capital at St. Petersburg on the Baltic Sea. He was consumed with the idea of westernizing Russia and forming ties with nations of Europe. The major cities and agricultural areas of Russia were developed in the European section. **Catherine II (the Great)** continued the process of modernizing and westernizing Russia. Her conquests added new territories in the Crimea and Poland, but Russia remained an insular, largely remote conglomeration of widely diverse cultural groups.

The absolutist tradition in Russian government has deep roots. **Ivan IV (the Terrible)**, who ruled Moscow in the Sixteenth Century took the title czar and is considered the founder of the Russian state. He ruled with an iron hand, relying on military power to eliminate rival princes and to subdue powerful landowners. Peter the Great and Catherine the Great continued the absolutist tradition, which remained unbroken until the **Bolshevik Revolution of 1917** and beyond. Czars ruled by divine right in a style similar to the French monarchs. When the liberal currents that swept Europe in the Nineteenth Century reached Russia, the czars reacted with characteristic repressive force. In 1905, Nicholas II crushed an attempted revolution, but he was unable to repeat this success in 1917 when the Bolsheviks seized control during Russia's tragic involvement in WWI.

Under the direction of **Lenin**, a Communist state based on the principles codified by **Marx** was instituted. Lenin adapted Marxist doctrine to the conditions in revolutionary Russia, and in the process, continued the absolutist tradition of the old czarist regime. Central to Lenin's scheme was the principle of **democratic centralism**, which stressed vertical decision-making within the Bolshevik/Communist Party. This system called for unwavering obedience from the lower echelons to the policies formulated at the top. Lenin also insisted on a well-disciplined and highly organized cadre of party professionals to interpret Marxist doctrine and to implement the Soviet system. The **Soviet Union** was established as a federation in 1922, and after Lenin died in 1924, **Joseph Stalin** emerged as the leader of the Communist Party and the Soviet state. He initiated a program of industrialization and collectivization of agriculture under the sometimes brutal **Five Year Plans**. Stalin consolidated his power with a series of **purges** that resulted in the execution or expulsion of thousands suspected of disloyalty. Stalin remained in power throughout WWII, after which the Soviet Union, despite tremendous human and economic losses, emerged as one of the two superpowers. Stalin's regime, though repressive, did succeed in raising the educational and technological levels of a previously backward, largely underdeveloped nation.

In the post-Stalinist period, **Nikita Khrushchev** and **Leonid Brezhnev** maintained the superpower status of the Soviet Union and held the system intact. In the 1980s, the Soviet Union became embroiled in a bitter, protracted war in **Afghanistan**. This action was the first Soviet military invasion of a sovereign nation outside of Eastern Europe. Soviet efforts to stave off a rebellion against the Marxist regime in Afghanistan were unsuccessful. Under **Mikhail Gorbachev**, who rose to power in the mid 1980s, the Soviets decided to withdraw their troops. Gorbachev was responsible for initiating a series of dramatic changes in the Soviet Union that ultimately toppled both himself and the whole Soviet system. These reforms included:

- **glasnost** – more individual freedom and a relaxation of censorship

- **perestroika** – a restructuring of the economy

- **democratization** – an attempt to provide voters with a choice of candidates in elections

An attempted coup in August 1991 led by Communist hardliners was put down largely due to the leadership of **Boris Yeltsin**, president of the Russian Republic. In December 1991, the Russian Parliament approved a plan backed by Yeltsin, now Gorbachev's rival, to set up a commonwealth of independent nations. The Soviet Union was dissolved, and Russia along with ten of the former Soviet republics formed the **Commonwealth of Independent States**. Gorbachev resigned as president of the Soviet Union. Boris Yeltsin, as President of Russia, was then recognized as the most powerful leader in the new configuration.

4.4.2 Government Structures and Functions

In the mid-1990s, the Russian Federation, the largest and most prominent of the Independent States, is governed under a constitution with a multi-party republican structure. The 1993 constitution assigned broad powers to the President, whose tenure is limited to two four year terms. The Parliament consists of the **Federation Council** (upper house) and the **State Duma** (lower house). Members of the Parliament are elected to four year terms. The government in the mid-1990s was still a work in progress.

Under the old Soviet system, a dualism existed with the government really a parallel structure to the powerful Communist Party. The government was organized as a separate entity, but significant posts were all filled by party hierarchy. The legislature (**Supreme Soviet**) was bicameral, consisting of the **Soviet of the Union** and the **Soviet of Nationalities**. Meeting twice a year, the Supreme Soviet's principal mission was to pass legislation drawn up by the leadership of the Communist Party. The thirty-nine member **Presidium** was headed by a chairman, who was recognized as the head of state. The Cabinet, or **Council of Ministers**, was the chief executive body of the government. Its ninety-odd members included the highest ranking officials of the Communist Party. They controlled foreign policy, economics, and cultural programs. The chairman of the Council of Ministers (**premier**) was the chief administrator of the Soviet Union. Stalin and Khrushchev served as both premier and head of the Communist Party simultaneously.

THE ORGANIZATION OF THE
COMMUNIST PARTY OF THE SOVIET UNION (1917-1991)

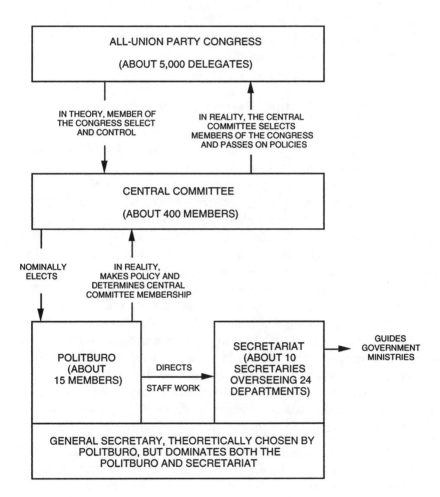

ALL-UNION PARTY CONGRESS

(ABOUT 5,000 DELEGATES)

IN THEORY, MEMBER OF THE CONGRESS SELECT AND CONTROL

IN REALITY, THE CENTRAL COMMITTEE SELECTS MEMBERS OF THE CONGRESS AND PASSES ON POLICIES

CENTRAL COMMITTEE

(ABOUT 400 MEMBERS)

NOMINALLY ELECTS

IN REALITY, MAKES POLICY AND DETERMINES CENTRAL COMMITTEE MEMBERSHIP

POLITBURO (ABOUT 15 MEMBERS)

DIRECTS

STAFF WORK

SECRETARIAT (ABOUT 10 SECRETARIES OVERSEEING 24 DEPARTMENTS)

GUIDES GOVERNMENT MINISTRIES

GENERAL SECRETARY, THEORETICALLY CHOSEN BY POLITBURO, BUT DOMINATES BOTH THE POLITBURO AND SECRETARIAT

Under Gorbachev's reform program, a **Congress of the USSR People's Deputies** to be elected by the people was instituted. This Congress of approximately 2,250 deputies was to select members of the Supreme Soviet. The Congress would also be responsible for choosing the President. The President's responsibilities included the formulation of foreign and defense policies and major legislative programs. The only President to serve under this system was Gorbachev himself. He resigned as both President of the Soviet Union and General Secretary of the Communist Party when the Commonwealth of Independent States was created.

4.4.3   Political Culture, Parties, and Participation

The population of the former Soviet Union included over one hundred ethnic groups with widely varying languages, religions, customs, and traditions. It is almost impossible to pigeonhole and categorize such a diverse mix or to describe it in terms of a particular political culture. Still some generalizations can be offered. Certainly the authoritarian and militaristic legacy of the old czarist regime could be detected in the Soviet brand of Communism with its totalitarian policies, elitist tendencies, and nuclear stockpiles. Soviet doctrine emphasized popular participation and egalitarianism, yet ordinary citizens were largely shut out of the policy-making process. Inherent divisions in Soviet society contributed to the lack of a coherent political culture. Different interests and agendas separated the peasants from the industrial laborers and the ordinary workers from the intelligentsia. The latter enjoyed high status privileges such as better apartments and access to consumer goods and services out of the reach of the agricultural and industrial classes. Ethnic, occupational, and intellectual divisions in Soviet society no doubt contributed to the dismantling of the communist systems.

During the seventy plus years that the Communist Party dominated, it served as a binding mechanism to hold the diverse and unwieldy elements of the Soviet society together. The party organization existed at three levels - local, republic, and national. On the local level, part-time volunteers with considerable responsibility headed the **Primary Party Organizations** (PPOs). Rank and file members were expected to adhere strictly to the party line and to serve as role models in the workplace and in the community. They were groomed from childhood in youth groups such as the **Little Octobrists** (ages 7–9), the **Young Pioneers** (ages 9–14), and the **Komsomol** or **League of Communist Youth**, an organization established by the Bolsheviks to train exemplary young men and women ages 14–28 to support the goals and methods of the new regime. The full-time paid professionals of the party elite were recruited from the foregoing groups and the schools and numbered upwards of one hundred thousand. They included the secretaries and the section chiefs of the party.

The Soviet government was dominated by the party with the elite firmly in control. Major policy decisions were made by the party's **Politburo**. It consisted of about fifteen members who met in secret, revealing only final decisions. The day-to-day work of the party was carried out by the members of the **Secretariat**. Traditionally the **General Secretary** of the Communist Party is also the leader of the Politburo. The organizational structure of the Soviet Communist Party is illustrated on the chart on page 61.

The once powerful Communist Party was outlawed with the restructuring of the government and the creation of the Commonwealth of Independent States in the early 1990s. A number of new parties, affiliations, and movements followed shortly thereafter, including a new and legal Communist Party. It remains to be seen if a distinctive civic culture will emerge in Russia and in the other members of the Commonwealth of Independent States. The Commonwealth suffers from a lack of cohesiveness due to fundamental conflicts over the allocation of military and economic resources. In Russia itself, ethnic conflicts are bound to erupt as seen in the rebel revolt in the breakaway state of Chechnya that broke out in 1995. Political instability will likely prevail so long as the economic crisis precipitated by the transition to a free market economy remains unresolved.

4.5　Government and Politics in the People's Republic of China

4.5.1　Geographic and Historical Context

The People's Republic of China, the world's most populous nation with over a billion inhabitants, is located in eastern Asia and is slightly larger than the United States in land mass. The name China, by which outsiders know the People's Republic, dates back to the Ch'in Dynasty, which unified the nation (221–207 BC) under the first emperor. The Chinese call their land Chung hua, or middle country, because the early peoples viewed their country as the middle of the world.

Modern China has clearly been shaped by a number of distinct historical forces including centuries of dynastic rule, control by foreigners during the imperialism of the Nineteenth Century, and the revolutionary currents of the twentieth century. Present Chinese political and cultural characteristics evolved from the legacy of these formative influences.

The origins of the Chinese dynastic system can be traced back to around 2000 BC when the inhabitants were concentrated in the Huang Ho basin. Rulers were powerful; obedience to authority was a given. **Confucianism**, a body of philosophical thought emphasizing order and harmony, reinforced the legitimacy of the dynastic system of government. A well-organized bureaucracy evolved where principal officials were selected for their skills and abilities as well as for their loyalty to the emperor. Sharp distinctions were drawn between the masses and the elite. Family and social relationships stressed order and obedience to higher authority similar to the pattern in the political sphere.

Famine and rebellion weakened the **Manchu Dynasty** in the nineteenth century paving the way for exploitation at the hands of foreign imperialists. Britain, France, Germany, Japan, and Russia carved out **spheres of influence** where each enjoyed exclusive trading privileges. As a result, foreigners were despised, and Chinese nationalists fomented rebellion. The Manchus were overthrown in

1911, and a weak republic was established. The idealistic Dr. Sun Yat-sen led the republicans. An era of **warlordism** followed during which local leaders vied for control, and instability was the rule.

Two distinct parties emerged from the chaos, the **Kuomintang (KMT)** and the **Chinese Communist Party (CCP)**. During the 1920s and 30s, the KMT sought to keep the warlords under control and worked for modernization and national unity. **Generalissimo Chiang Kai-shek** emerged as the leader of the **Nationalists (KMT)**. The CCP, under the control of the charismatic **Mao Zedong (Mao Tse-tung)**, in contrast, stressed economic and social reform. The two groups engaged in a bloody struggle that culminated with Mao's forces embarking on the legendary **Long March** (1934–1935). They fled to northwestern China hotly pursued by Chiang's Nationalist forces. The survivors were joined by fresh recruits, and together they refined CCP doctrine and prepared for the struggle ahead.

Due to Japanese aggression against China throughout the 1930s, the Nationalists and the Communists formed a temporary united front. Together they resisted a common enemy, but with the conclusion of WWII in 1945, hostilities between the two groups resumed. Civil war raged in China until 1949 when the CCP triumphed. Chiang and the Nationalists were driven off the mainland to **Taiwan** where they formed their own government. The CCP took control of mainland China and established the People's Republic.

Under the leadership of Mao Zedong, a style of Communism evolved that reflected, in part, China's ancient heritage but also incorporated Chairman Mao's original contributions to the body of Marxist/Leninist thought. These include the following revisions:

- An emphasis on the **peasantry** as the principal revolutionary force rather than the urban proletariat identified by Marx.

- A **mass line** policy that recognized the contributions that could be made by both peasants and other common laborers to the formulation of party practice. Mao's mass line both contrasted with and complemented Lenin's democratic centralism.

- The concept that theory must be put to the test in practical situations to avoid esoteric doctrine divorced from the realities of everyday life.

- A recognition that society is constantly evolving and in danger of falling into old bourgeois habits. Mao believed such relapses must be avoided whatever the cost.

- The practice of reforming thought through indoctrination with the state as an instrument of moral persuasion. This concept is rooted in China's early dynastic tradition.

During Mao's tenure, two major programs were instituted with mixed results. These were the **Great Leap Forward** (1958–1960) and the **Cultural Revolution** (1966–1969). The Great Leap was an economic campaign that differed from Mao's earlier Soviet-inspired Five Year Plan, which stressed the development of heavy industry at the expense of agriculture. Mao's Great Leap, on the other hand, emphasized mass mobilization for modernization in industry with "backyard furnaces" and more local control. Central to the Great Leap was the communization of agriculture. These economic innovations did not succeed to the extent that the government hoped. In the mid-1960s, largely in response to criticism of the Great Leap, the Cultural Revolution was launched. This movement went far beyond economics in its goal to root out corruptive influences and to restore the zeal of the original revolution. The youthful, zealous **Red Guards** went so far overboard in their attacks against suspected traitors and elitist factions that the People's Liberation Army had to be summoned to restore order.

In 1976 both Mao and the more moderate **Zhou En-lai** passed away and an era of modernization was initiated. **Deng Xiaoping** and the moderates embarked on a flexible program of reform that combined both Maoist strategies and foreign innovations. Bitter factions struggled for influence, the most notorious being the rabidly Maoist **Gang of Four**, which was led by Mao's widow, **Jiang Qing**. They were later arrested and expelled from the CCP. Under the leadership of Deng, agriculture was decollectivized, private business ventures were permitted, and students were allowed to study abroad. When the **Democracy Movement** rallied in **Tiananmen Square** in 1989, however, it was forcefully suppressed by the People's Liberation Army. Liberalization under Deng did not go so far as to embrace democratic political values.

4.5.2 Government Structures and Functions

The government of the People's Republic of China was patterned after the Soviet model. Several constitutions have been written over the life of the Communist state to reflect changes in CCP policy. The 1982 constitution was created to stabilize the government after the death of Mao Zedong.

Legislative power is vested in the **National People's Congress** and the **Standing Committee of the Congress**. With nearly three thousand deputies, the National People's Congress is, in theory, the highest organ of the state. It is slated to meet annually, but this is not always the case. The National People's Congress symbolizes the broad base of state power. The much smaller Standing Committee is in session year round passing legislation and selecting such officials as the President, Premier, and various ministers. The head of state is the President. This largely ceremonial post was eliminated in the 1975 constitution but reinstated in 1982. The **State Council Cabinet**, the highest administrative organ, is comprised of commissioners and ministers. It is headed by the **Premier**. The officials in the State Council belong to the CCP and are responsible for translating party decisions into state policy.

At lower levels, urban and village committees form the popular base of the governmental structure. A series of administrative units form a pyramid-like pattern. **People's Congresses** govern at the provincial level and also administer the autonomous border regions. The national government in **Beijing** sits at the top of the pyramid.

4.5.3 Political Culture, Party, and Participation

The principal political force in the People's Republic of China is the Communist Party. In structure it roughly parallels the state system of government. The hierarchical organization of the party ostensibly begins at the local cells and moves up through a series of units at various levels culminating with the **National Party Congress**, whose members are chosen by local and provincial congresses. Its primary function is to select the **Central Committee of the People's Republic**. The Central Committee in turn chooses the members of the **Politburo** and the **Secretariat**, both of which are headed by the **Secretary General**. Despite Mao's mass line theory, as in the Soviet Union, power flows from the top down. The CCP does suggest that party leaders at lower levels communicate with the masses and pass along their sentiments to party leaders. Despite this system, democratic centralism, with its emphasis on adherence to party policy, is the rule.

Prior to the 1982 constitution, the Chairman of the CCP occupied the highest office in the land. The new constitution eliminated the position in an effort to discourage the concentration of unlimited power in the hands of one individual. The chairmanship was replaced by the administrative post of Secretary General. A **Central Advisory Commission** was created to provide advice and assistance to the Central Committee of the CCP. In an attempt to encourage aging party members to remain active, only those with many years of service were invited to be on the Advisory Commission.

In theory, anyone in China over 18 years of age who is willing to work for the CCP and to serve as a role model can join. As a member of the CCP, one must accept party discipline and remain active. Fulltime paid workers or **cadres** form the foundation of the CCP network. Young leaders are recruited from the **Communist Youth League**. By the late 1980s, the CCP had 47 million members.

A unique organ of the Chinese political culture is the **People's Liberation Army**. The early Communists engaged in years of armed struggle to overcome the Nationalists and to institute their regime. Hence the army was regarded as an essential component in the institutionalization of the Communist system. Leaders of the army are at the same time leaders of the party, and as such they contribute to the policy-making process.

The Chinese Communist Party continues on an ambivalent course of encouraging capitalist economic programs while remaining faithful to one-party rule and ideological purity. Human rights abuses remain an issue of contention between China and the international community. The brutal suppression of the pro-democracy demonstration in Tiananmen Square, the one-child per family forced abortion policy, and the continuing inferior status of women are but a few of the indications that, despite protestations to the contrary, China has not liberalized its social policy. Another potential source for instability in the People's Republic is the absence of a well-defined mechanism for orderly political succession.

CHAPTER 5

International Relations

5.1 The Theoretical Framework

The study of how nations interact with one another can be approached from a variety of perspectives including the following:

- A **traditional analysis** uses the descriptive process and focuses on such topics as global issues, international institutions, and the foreign policies of individual nation states.

- The **strategists' approach** zeroes in on war and deterrence. Scholars in this camp may employ game theory to analyze negotiations, the effectiveness of weapons systems, and the likelihood of limited vs. all-out war in a given crisis situation.

- The **middle range theorists** analyze specific components of international relations, such as the politics of arms races, the escalation of international crises, and the role of prejudice and attitudes toward other cultures in precipitating war and peace.

- A **world politics approach** takes into consideration such factors as economics, ethics, law, and trade agreements and stresses the significance of international organizations and the complexities of interactions among nations.

- The **grand theory** of international relations is presented by **Hans J. Morgenthau** in *Politics Among Nations* (1948). He argues for **realism** in the study of interactions on the international stage. Morgenthau suggests that an analysis of relations among nations reveals such recurring themes as "interest defined as power" and striving for equilibrium/balance of power as a means of maintaining peace.

- The **idealists** assume that human nature is essentially good, hence people and nations are capable of cooperation and avoiding armed conflict. They highlight global organizations, international law, disarmament, and the reform of institutions that lead to war.

An analysis of international politics can be conducted at various levels by looking at the actions of individual statesmen, the interests of individual nations, and/or the mechanics of a whole system of international players. In studying the rise of Nazism and its role in precipitating WWII, the **individual** approach would focus on Hitler, the **state** approach would treat the German preoccupation with racial superiority and the need for expansion, and the **systemic** approach would highlight how German military campaigns upset the balance of power and triggered unlikely alliances, such as the linking of the democratic Britain and the United States with the totalitarian Soviet Union in a common effort to restore equilibrium.

5.2   Foreign Policy Perspectives

International relations as a discipline is inextricably linked to the field of **foreign policy**. Foreign policy involves the objectives nations seek to gain with reference to other nations and the procedures in which they engage in order to achieve their objectives. The principal foreign policy goals of sovereign states or other political entities may include some or all of the following: independence, national security, economic advancement, encouraging their political values beyond their own borders, gaining respect and prestige, and promoting stability and international peace.

The **foreign policy process** involves the stages a government goes through in formulating policy and arriving at decisions with respect to courses of action. A variety of models have been identified in reference to the process of creating foreign policy. The **primary players** (nations, world organizations, multinational corporations, and non-state ethnic entities such as the Palestine Liberation Organization) are often referred to as **actors**.

The **unitary/rational actor model** assumes that all nations or primary players share similar goals and approach foreign policy issues in like fashion. The actions players take, according to this theory, are influenced by the actions of other players rather than by what may be taking place internally. The rational component in this model is based on the assumption that actors will respond on the world stage by making the best choice after measured consideration of possible alternatives. Maximizing goals and achieving specific objectives motivate the rational actor's course of action.

The **bureaucratic model** assumes that, due to the many large organizations involved in formulating foreign policy, particularly in powerful nation states, final decisions are the result of struggle among the bureaucratic actors. In the United States, the bureaucratic actors include the Departments of State and Defense, as well as the National Security Council, the Central Intelligence Agency, the Environmental Protection Agency, the Department of Commerce, and/or any other agencies and departments whose agendas might be impacted by a foreign policy decision. While the bureaucratic model is beneficial in that it assumes the consideration of multiple points of view, the downside is that inter-agency competition and compromise often drive the final decision.

A third model assumes that foreign policy results from the intermingling of a variety of political factors including national leaders, bureaucratic organizations, legislative bodies, political parties, interest groups, and public opinion.

The **implementation of foreign policy** depends upon the tools a nation or primary player has at its disposal. The major instruments of foreign policy include **diplomacy**, **military strength/actions**, and **economic initiatives**.

Diplomacy involves communicating with other primary players through official representatives. It might include attending conferences and summit meetings, negotiating treaties and settlements, and exchanging official communications. Diplomacy is an indispensable tool in the successful conduct of an entity's foreign policy.

The extent to which a player may rely on the **military** tool depends upon its technological strength, its readiness, and the support of both its domestic population and the international community. President Bush's decision to engage in a military conflict with Iraq's Saddam Hussein in 1991 largely rested on positive assessments of the aforementioned factors. Sometimes the buildup of military capabilities is in itself a powerful foreign policy tool and a deterrent to armed conflict as was the case in the Cold War between the United States and the Soviet Union.

Economic development and the ability to employ economic initiatives to achieve foreign policy objectives are effective means by which a principal player can interact on the international scene. The Marshall Plan, through which the United States provided economic aid to a ravaged Europe after WWII, could be viewed as a tool to block Soviet expansion as well as a humanitarian gesture. It was a tool to resurrect the devastated economies of Europe which had been major trading partners and purchasers of U.S. exports before the war. Membership in an economic community such as OPEC (Organization of Petroleum Exporting Countries) or the EC (European Community) can drive the foreign policy of both member nations and those impacted by their decisions.

5.3   The Modern Global System

International systems today evidence many of the global forces and foreign policy mechanisms formulated in Western Europe in the Eighteenth and Nineteenth Centuries. Largely due to the influence of Western imperialism and colonialism, the less developed countries of modern times have, to a great extent, embraced ideological and foreign policy values that originated in Europe during the formative centuries. Such concepts as political autonomy, nationalism, economic advancement through technology and industrialization, and gaining respect and prestige in the international community move the foreign policies of major powers and many less developed countries as well.

5.3.1 Historical Context of Modern Global System

The modern global system or network of relationships among nations owes its origins to the emergence of the nation-state. It is generally recognized that the **Peace of Westphalia (1648)**, which concluded the Thirty Years War in Europe and ended the authority of the Roman Catholic popes to exert their political dominance over secular leaders, gave birth to the concept of the modern nation-state. The old feudal order in Europe that allowed the Holy Roman Emperor to extend his influence over the territories governed by local princes was replaced by a new one in which distinct geographic and political entities interacted under a new set of principles. These allowed the nation-states to conduct business with each other, such as negotiating treaties and settling border disputes, without interference from a higher authority. Hence the concept of sovereignty evolved.

The Eighteenth Century in Europe was notable for its relatively even distribution of power among the nation-states. With respect to military strength and international prestige, such nations as England, France, Austria, Prussia, and Russia were on the same scale. Some of the former major powers, such as Spain, the Netherlands, and Portugal occupied a secondary status. Both the major and secondary players created alliances and competed with each other for control of territories beyond their borders. Alignments, based primarily on economic and colonial considerations, shifted without upsetting the global system. Royal families intermarried and professional soldiers worked for the states that gave them the best benefits without great regard for political allegiances.

Military conflicts in the Eighteenth Century tended to be conservative with the concept of the **balance of power** at play. Mercenaries and professionals controlled the action mindful of strategic maneuvers to bring about victory. Wiping out the enemy was not the principal goal. Major upheavals were avoided through the formation of alliances and a high regard for the authority of monarchs and the Christian Church. The Eighteenth Century has been dubbed the **"golden age of diplomacy"** because it was an era of relative stability where moderation and shared cultural values on the part of the decision-makers were the rule.

Structural changes in the process and implementation of international relations occurred in the Nineteenth and Twentieth Centuries due to major political, technological, and ideological developments.

The nation-state of the Eighteenth Century was a relatively new phenomenon. Statesmen of the era traded territory with little consideration of ethnic loyalties. This style of diplomacy was irrevocably altered by the French Revolution and the Napoleonic Wars that saw **nationality** emerge as a rallying point for conducting wars and for raising the citizens' armies necessary to succeed in military conflicts. The trend was exacerbated in the mid-Nineteenth Century by the European drive for unification of distinct ethnic groups and the creation of the Italian and German nation-states. The Twentieth Century has seen a particularly impassioned link between nationalism and war.

The scientific and industrial revolutions of the Eighteenth Century gave rise to advancements in **military technology** in the Nineteenth and Twentieth Centuries that dramatically altered the concept and the conduct of war. Replacing the Eighteenth Century conservative, play-by-the-rules approach was a new, fiercely violent brand of warfare that increasingly involved civilian casualties and aimed at utter destruction of the enemy. The World Wars of the Twentieth Century called for mass mobilization of civilians as well as of the military, prompting leaders to whip up nationalistic sentiments. The development of nuclear weapons in the Mid-Twentieth Century rendered total war largely unfeasible. Nuclear arms buildups, with the goal of **deterrent capabilities** (the means to retaliate so swiftly and effectively that an enemy will avoid conflict) was viewed by the superpowers as the only safety net.

Another factor molding the structural changes in international relations that surfaced in the Nineteenth and Twentieth Centuries was the **ideological component**. Again the French Revolution, anchored in the ideology of "liberty, equality, and fraternity," is viewed as the harbinger of future trends. Those conservative forces valuing legitimacy and monarchy fought the forces of the Revolution and Napoleon to preserve tradition against the rising tide of republican nationalism. In the Twentieth Century, with its binding "isms" - Communism, democratic republicanism, liberalism, Nazism, socialism - competing for dominance, ideological conflicts have become more pronounced.

5.3.2 The Contemporary Global System

The values of the contemporary system are rooted in the currents of Eighteenth and Nineteenth century Europe, transplanted to the rest of the world through colonialism and imperialism. The forces of nationalism, belief in technological progress, and ideological motivations, as well as the desire for international respect and prestige, are evident world-wide. Principal players in Africa, Asia, Latin America, and the Middle East as often as not dominate the diplomatic arena.

The contemporary scene in international relations is comprised of a number of entities beyond the **nation-state**. These include: **non-state actors** or **principal players, nonterritorial transnational organizations** and **nonterritorial intergovernmental** or **multinational organizations.**

Contemporary **nation-states** are legal entities occupying well-defined geographic areas and organized under a common set of governmental institutions. They are recognized by other members of the international community as sovereign and independent states.

Non-state actors or **principal players** are movements or parties that function as independent states. They lack sovereignty, but they may actually wield more power than some less developed nation-states. The **Palestine Liberation Organization (PLO)** is an example of a non-state actor that conducts its own foreign policy, purchases armaments, and has committed acts of terror with grave consequences for the contemporary international community. The **Irish Republican Army (IRA)** is another example of a non-state actor that has employed systematic acts of terror to achieve political ends.

Nonterritorial transitional organizations are institutions such as the Catholic Church that conduct activities throughout the world but whose aims are largely nonpolitical. A relatively new nonterritorial transnational organization is the **multi-national corporation (MNC)**, such as General Motors, Hitachi, or British Petroleum. These giant business entities have bases in a number of countries and exist primarily for economic profit. Despite their apparent nonpolitical agendas, multinational corporations can greatly impact foreign policy, as in the case of the United Fruit Company's suspect complicity in the overthrow of the government of Guatemala in the 1950s. Initially the MNC was largely an American innovation, but in recent years, Asian players, particularly the Japanese, have proliferated, changing the makeup of the scene.

An **intergovernmental organization**, such as the United Nations, NATO, or the European Community, is made up of nation-states and can wield significant power on the international scene. While NATO is primarily a military intergovernmental organization, and the EC is mainly economic, the UN is really a multipurpose entity. While its primary mission is to promote world peace, the UN engages in a variety of social, cultural, economic, health, and humanitarian activities.

The contemporary global system tends to classify nation-states based on power, wealth, and prestige in the international community. Such labels as **superpower, secondary power, middle power, small power**, and the like tend to be confusing because they are not based on a single set of criteria or a shared set of standards. Some countries may be strong militarily, as was Iraq prior to the Persian Gulf War, yet lack the wealth and prestige in the international community to classify them as super or secondary powers. Others like Japan may have little military capabilities, but wide influence due to economic preeminence.

The **structure** of the contemporary global system during the Cold War was distinctly **bipolar**, with the United States and the Soviet Union assuming diplomatic, ideological, and military leadership for the international community. With the breakup of the Soviet Union and the reorganization of the Eastern bloc countries has come the disintegration of the bipolar system. Since the 1970s, when tensions between the United States and the Soviet Union eased, a **multipolar system**, in which new alignments are flexible and more easily drawn, has been emerging. President Bush spoke of the **New World Order** at the end of the Cold War. This concept involves alliances that transcend the old bipolar scheme with its emphasis on ideology and military superiority and calls for multinational cooperation as seen in the Persian Gulf War. It also assumes greater non-military, transnational cooperation in scientific research and humanitarian projects. The multipolar system is less cohesive than the bipolar system of the recent past and the orders of the distant past, such as the **hierarchical system** (one unit dominates) of the Holy Roman Empire or the **diffuse system** (power and influence are distributed among a large number of units) of Eighteenth Century Europe.

A set of fundamental rules has long governed international relations and, though often ignored, is still held as the standard today. These rules include **territorial integrity, sovereignty,** and the **legal equality of nation-states.** However, in an age of covert operations, mass media, multinational corporations, and shifting territorial boundaries, these traditional rules of international conduct are subject to both violation and revision.

5.4   International Law

The present system of international law is rooted in the fundamental rules of global relations: territorial integrity, sovereignty, and legal equality of nation-states. It embodies a set of basic principles mandating what countries may or may not do and under what conditions the rules should be applied.

5.4.1   Historical Context

Despite evidence that the legal and ethical norms of modern international law may have guided interactions among political entities in non-Western pre-industrial systems, contemporary international law emanates from the Western legal traditions of Greece, Rome, and modern Europe. The development of the European nation-state gave rise to a system of legal rights and responsibilities in the international sphere that enlarged upon the religious-based code of the feudal era. In medieval Europe, the church's emphasis on hierarchical obligations, duty, and obedience to authority helped shape the notion of the **"just war." Hugo Grotius** (1583–1645), Dutch scholar and statesman, codified the laws of war and peace and has been called the **"father of international law."**

A new era was launched in 1648, with the Peace of Westphalia, that promulgated the idea of the treaty as the basis of international law. Multilateral treaties dominated the Eighteenth century, while Britain, with its unparalleled sea power, established and enforced maritime law. By the Nineteenth Century, advances in military technology rendered the old standard of the "just war" obsolete. Deterrents, rather than legal and ethical principles, provided the means to a relatively stable world order. The concept of **neutrality** evolved during this period, defining the rights and responsibilities of both warring and neutral nations. These restraints helped prevent smaller conflicts from erupting into world wars.

5.4.2 Contemporary International Law

In the Twentieth Century, international law has retreated theoretically from the tradition of using force as a legitimate tool for settling international conflicts. The **Covenant of the League of Nations** (1920), the **Kellogg-Briand Pact** (1929), and the **United Nations Charter** (1945) all emphasize peaceful relations among nations, but the use of force continues to be employed to achieve political ends. The **International Court of Justice**, the judicial arm of the United Nations and its predecessor, the **Permanent Court of International Justice** represent concerted efforts to replace armed conflict with the rule of law. Unfortunately the World Court has proven to be an ineffective organ. Nation-states are reluctant to submit vital questions to the Court, and there is a lack of consensus as to the norms to be applied. Members of the United Nations are members of the Court, but they are not compelled to submit their international disputes for consideration.

The UN Charter seeks to humanize the international scene in its admonition that all member nations assist victims of aggression. This approach negates the old idea of neutrality. It further dismisses the tradition of war as a legitimate tool for resolution of disputes between nation-states of equal legal status. Aggressive conflicts can be categorized as crimes against humanity, and individuals may be held personally accountable for launching them.

The concept of international law has been criticized on several fronts. The rise of **multiculturalism**, with its emphasis on multiple perspectives, has called into question the relevance of applying Western legal traditions to the global community. International law has been seen as an instrument of the powerful nations in pursuit of their aims at the expense of weaker nations. Strong nation-states are in a position to both enforce international law and to violate it without fear of reprisal. These observations have led some to conclude that international law is primarily an instrument to maintain the **status quo**.

International law can be effective if parties involved see some **mutual self-advantage** in compliance. **Fear of reprisal** is another factor influencing nations to observe the tenets of international law. **Diplomatic advantage** and **enhanced global prestige** may follow a nation's decisions to abide by international law. It can be argued that international law is valuable in that it seeks to impose **order** on a potentially chaotic system and sets expectations that, while not always met, are positive and affirming.

Available at your local bookstore or order directly from us by sending in coupon below.

Available at your local bookstore or order directly from us by sending in coupon below.

The Best Test Preparation for the

LSAT
Law School Admission Test

6 FULL-LENGTH EXAMS
written by test experts

Completely Up-to-Date Based on the Current Format of the LSAT

plus **COMPLETE COACHING & REVIEW COURSE**

LSAT Exercise Drills For All Test Sections

LSAT Study Course Schedule

*PLUS...*expert test tips and strategies for answering the different types of questions found on the exam — to help you achieve a **TOP SCORE**

RE**A** *Research & Education Association*

Available at your local bookstore or order directly from us by sending in coupon below.

Available at your local bookstore or order directly from us by sending in coupon below.

"The ESSENTIALS"
of HISTORY

REA's **Essentials of History** series offers a new approach to the study of history that is different from what has been available previously. Compared with conventional history outlines, the **Essentials of History** offer far more detail, with fuller explanations and interpretations of historical events and developments. Compared with voluminous historical tomes and textbooks, the **Essentials of History** offer a far more concise, less ponderous overview of each of the periods they cover.

The **Essentials of History** provide quick access to needed information, and will serve as handy reference sources at all times. The **Essentials of History** are prepared with REA's customary concern for high professional quality and student needs.

UNITED STATES HISTORY
1500 to 1789 From Colony to Republic
1789 to 1841 The Developing Nation
1841 to 1877 Westward Expansion & the Civil War
1877 to 1912 Industrialism, Foreign Expansion & the Progressive Era
1912 to 1941 World War I, the Depression & the New Deal
America since 1941: Emergence as a World Power

WORLD HISTORY
Ancient History (4500 BC to AD 500)
The Emergence of Western Civilization
Medieval History (AD 500 to 1450)
The Middle Ages

EUROPEAN HISTORY
1450 to 1648 The Renaissance, Reformation & Wars of Religion
1648 to 1789 Bourbon, Baroque & the Enlightenment
1789 to 1848 Revolution & the New European Order
1848 to 1914 Realism & Materialism
1914 to 1935 World War I & Europe in Crisis
Europe since 1935: From World War II to the Demise of Communism

CANADIAN HISTORY
Pre-Colonization to 1867
The Beginning of a Nation
1867 to Present
The Post-Confederate Nation

If you would like more information about any of these books,
complete the coupon below and return it to us or visit your local bookstore.

MAXnotes®

REA's Literature Study Guides

MAXnotes® are student-friendly. They offer a fresh look at masterpieces of literature, presented in a lively and interesting fashion. **MAXnotes®** offer the essentials of what you should know about the work, including outlines, explanations and discussions of the plot, character lists, analyses, and historical context. **MAXnotes®** are designed to help you think independently about literary works by raising various issues and thought-provoking ideas and questions. Written by literary experts who currently teach the subject, **MAXnotes®** enhance your understanding and enjoyment of the work.

Available **MAXnotes®** include the following:

Absalom, Absalom!	Henry IV, Part I	Othello
The Aeneid of Virgil	Henry V	Paradise
Animal Farm	The House on Mango Street	Paradise Lost
Antony and Cleopatra	Huckleberry Finn	A Passage to India
As I Lay Dying	I Know Why the Caged	Plato's Republic
As You Like It	Bird Sings	Portrait of a Lady
The Autobiography of	The Iliad	A Portrait of the Artist
Malcolm X	Invisible Man	as a Young Man
The Awakening	Jane Eyre	Pride and Prejudice
Beloved	Jazz	A Raisin in the Sun
Beowulf	The Joy Luck Club	Richard II
Billy Budd	Jude the Obscure	Romeo and Juliet
The Bluest Eye, A Novel	Julius Caesar	The Scarlet Letter
Brave New World	King Lear	Sir Gawain and the
The Canterbury Tales	Leaves of Grass	Green Knight
The Catcher in the Rye	Les Misérables	Slaughterhouse-Five
The Color Purple	Lord of the Flies	Song of Solomon
The Crucible	Macbeth	The Sound and the Fury
Death in Venice	The Merchant of Venice	The Stranger
Death of a Salesman	Metamorphoses of Ovid	Sula
Dickens Dictionary	Metamorphosis	The Sun Also Rises
The Divine Comedy I: Inferno	Middlemarch	A Tale of Two Cities
Dubliners	A Midsummer Night's Dream	The Taming of the Shrew
The Edible Woman	Moby-Dick	Tar Baby
Emma	Moll Flanders	The Tempest
Euripides' Medea & Electra	Mrs. Dalloway	Tess of the D'Urbervilles
Frankenstein	Much Ado About Nothing	Their Eyes Were Watching God
Gone with the Wind	Mules and Men	Things Fall Apart
The Grapes of Wrath	My Antonia	To Kill a Mockingbird
Great Expectations	Native Son	To the Lighthouse
The Great Gatsby	1984	Twelfth Night
Gulliver's Travels	The Odyssey	Uncle Tom's Cabin
Handmaid's Tale	Oedipus Trilogy	Waiting for Godot
Hamlet	Of Mice and Men	Wuthering Heights
Hard Times	On the Road	Guide to Literary Terms
Heart of Darkness		

REA's Problem Solvers

The "PROBLEM SOLVERS" are comprehensive supplemental textbooks designed to save time in finding solutions to problems. Each "PROBLEM SOLVER" is the first of its kind ever produced in its field. It is the product of a massive effort to illustrate almost any imaginable problem in exceptional depth, detail, and clarity. Each problem is worked out in detail with a step-by-step solution, and the problems are arranged in order of complexity from elementary to advanced. Each book is fully indexed for locating problems rapidly.

ACCOUNTING
ADVANCED CALCULUS
ALGEBRA & TRIGONOMETRY
AUTOMATIC CONTROL
  SYSTEMS/ROBOTICS
BIOLOGY
BUSINESS, ACCOUNTING, & FINANCE
CALCULUS
CHEMISTRY
COMPLEX VARIABLES
DIFFERENTIAL EQUATIONS
ECONOMICS
ELECTRICAL MACHINES
ELECTRIC CIRCUITS
ELECTROMAGNETICS
ELECTRONIC COMMUNICATIONS
ELECTRONICS
FINITE & DISCRETE MATH
FLUID MECHANICS/DYNAMICS
GENETICS
GEOMETRY
HEAT TRANSFER

LINEAR ALGEBRA
MACHINE DESIGN
MATHEMATICS for ENGINEERS
MECHANICS
NUMERICAL ANALYSIS
OPERATIONS RESEARCH
OPTICS
ORGANIC CHEMISTRY
PHYSICAL CHEMISTRY
PHYSICS
PRE-CALCULUS
PROBABILITY
PSYCHOLOGY
STATISTICS
STRENGTH OF MATERIALS &
  MECHANICS OF SOLIDS
TECHNICAL DESIGN GRAPHICS
THERMODYNAMICS
TOPOLOGY
TRANSPORT PHENOMENA
VECTOR ANALYSIS

If you would like more information about any of these books, complete the coupon below and return it to us or visit your local bookstore.

RESEARCH & EDUCATION ASSOCIATION
61 Ethel Road W. • Piscataway, New Jersey 08854
Phone: (732) 819-8880   **website: www.rea.com**

Please send me more information about your Problem Solver books

Name _____

Address _____

City _____ State _____ Zip _____

REA's Test Preps
The Best in Test Preparation

- REA "Test Preps" are **far more** comprehensive than any other test preparation series
- Each book contains up to **eight** full-length practice tests based on the most recent exams
- **Every** type of question likely to be given on the exams is included
- Answers are accompanied by **full** and **detailed** explanations

REA publishes over 60 Test Preparation volumes in several series. They include:

Advanced Placement Exams (APs)
Biology
Calculus AB & Calculus BC
Chemistry
Computer Science
English Language & Composition
English Literature & Composition
European History
Government & Politics
Physics
Psychology
Spanish Language
Statistics
United States History

College-Level Examination Program (CLEP)
Analyzing and Interpreting Literature
College Algebra
Freshman College Composition
General Examinations
General Examinations Review
History of the United States I
Human Growth and Development
Introductory Sociology
Principles of Marketing
Spanish

SAT II: Subject Tests
Biology E/M
Chemistry
English Language Proficiency Test
French
German
Literature

SAT II: Subject Tests (cont'd)
Mathematics Level IC, IIC
Physics
Spanish
United States History
Writing

Graduate Record Exams (GREs)
Biology
Chemistry
Computer Science
General
Literature in English
Mathematics
Physics
Psychology

ACT - ACT Assessment

ASVAB - Armed Services Vocational Aptitude Battery

CBEST - California Basic Educational Skills Test

CDL - Commercial Driver License Exam

CLAST - College-Level Academic Skills Test

ELM - Entry Level Mathematics

ExCET - Exam for the Certification of Educators in Texas

FE (EIT) - Fundamentals of Engineering Exam

FE Review - Fundamentals of Engineering Review

GED - High School Equivalency Diploma Exam (U.S. & Canadian editions)

GMAT - Graduate Management Admission Test

LSAT - Law School Admission Test

MAT - Miller Analogies Test

MCAT - Medical College Admission Test

MTEL - Massachusetts Tests for Educator Licensure

MSAT - Multiple Subjects Assessment for Teachers

NJ HSPA - New Jersey High School Proficiency Assessment

PLT - Principles of Learning & Teaching Tests

PPST - Pre-Professional Skills Tests

PSAT - Preliminary Scholastic Assessment Test

SAT I - Reasoning Test

SAT I - Quick Study & Review

TASP - Texas Academic Skills Program

TOEFL - Test of English as a Foreign Language

TOEIC - Test of English for International Communication

RESEARCH & EDUCATION ASSOCIATION
61 Ethel Road W. • Piscataway, New Jersey 08854
Phone: (732) 819-8880   **website: www.rea.com**

Please send me more information about your Test Prep books

Name _____

Address _____

City _____ State _____ Zip _____